# Christmas
in
# My Heart

STORIES TO SHARE
THE SPIRIT OF THE SEASON

❖

*Christmas*

*in*

*My Heart*

A FOURTH TREASURY

❖

*Compiled and Edited by*

JOE WHEELER

*Doubleday*

NEW YORK  LONDON  TORONTO

SYDNEY  AUCKLAND

PUBLISHED BY DOUBLEDAY
a division of Random House, Inc.
1540 Broadway, New York, New York 10036

DOUBLEDAY and the portrayal of an anchor with
a dolphin are registered trademarks of Doubleday,
a division of Random House, Inc.

*Book design by Jennifer Ann Daddio*

Woodcut illustrations are from
the library of Joe Wheeler.

The Illustration on page 40 appears courtesy of Michael David Biegel.

Library of Congress Cataloging-in-Publication Data
Christmas in My heart. Selections
Christmas in my heart: a fourth treasury: further
tales of holiday joy / compiled and edited by
Joe Wheeler.—1st ed.
p.    cm.
Short stories chiefly selected from the volumes of
*Christmas in My Heart* published by Review and Herald
Pub. Association, c1922–c1996.
1. Christmas stories, American.    I. Wheeler, Joe L.,
1936–    .    II. Title.
PS648.C45C4472 1998
813'.0108334—dc21    98-16727
CIP

ISBN 0-385-49318-5
Copyright © 1999 by Joe Wheeler
All Rights Reserved
Printed in the United States of America
October 1999
First Edition

3  5  7  9  10  8  6  4  2

*Barbara Leininger Wheller*

My beloved mother it was who set my sails for life,
passing on to me, during preschool years
and eight years of home schooling,
a great love and appreciation for the
Judeo-Christian stories that touch the heart.
Because of this, these are her stories too.

# Acknowledgments

Introduction: "A Pennsylvania Deutsch Christmas," by Joe Wheeler. Copyright © 1995 (Revised, 1999). Printed by permission of the author.

"A String of Blue Beads," by Fulton Oursler. Copyright © 1951 by Reader's Digest Association, Inc. Used by permission of Doubleday, Dell, Bantam.

"Bethany's Christmas Carol," by Mabel McKee. Printed by permission of Fleming H. Revell, a division of Baker Book House.

"Joey's Miracle," by Hartley F. Dailey. Copyright © 1995. Printed by permission of the author.

"And It Was Christmas Morning," by Temple Bailey. If anyone can provide knowledge of earliest publication and date of this old story, please relay this information to Joe Wheeler, care of Doubleday Religion Department.

"Delayed Delivery," by Cathy Miller. Published in *Northern Life*, December 26, 1992, Sudbury, Ontario, Canada. Printed by permission of the author.

"The Tallest Angel." Author and original source unknown. If anyone can provide knowledge of authorship, origin, and first publication source of this old story, please relay this information to Joe Wheeler, care of Doubleday Religion Department.

"Truce in the Forest," by Fritz Vincken. Reprinted with permission from the January 1973 *Reader's Digest*. Copyright © 1973 by the Reader's Digest Association, Inc.

"Pink Angel." Author and original source unknown. If anyone can provide knowledge of the authorship, origin, and first publication source of this old story, please relay this

# Contents

# A Pennsylvania Deutsch Christmas

❖

## INTRODUCTION:

*With this fourth collection, I'd like to take you on a journey with me, as exciting a journey as I've ever taken: a journey into my own past.*

*Actually, it all started not long ago, when I attended my first ever Leininger* family reunion, held in a very old Lutheran churchyard in the Blue Mountains of Pennsylvania. I was so moved by the experience that I determined to find out more about my German roots. As fate would have it, sitting next to me at that reunion was a distant cousin, Richard Leininger Pawling, who is a specialist in living history. And one of his specialties is Pennsylvania Deutsch history. What we label Dutch is an American transformation of the German word *Deutsch,* which means German.

When my new-found cousin discovered my own interest in Christmas traditions, he promised—and followed up on it—to send me a packet of Pennsylvania German Christmas history. Later on, the editors of the American Society of Germans from Russia, in Lincoln, Nebraska, sent me another. And another distant cousin, Dr. Thomas Leininger, has helped to fill in more of the missing pieces of Pennsylvania German history. Out of this treasure chest of Christmas history I have been able to make possible this brief journey into the past, through which we discover the beginnings of such familiar traditions as the Christmas card, the Christmas tree, Saint Nicholas, Christkindel, along with wonderful food and stirring music.

. . .

German migration to America started in earnest when William Penn invited his continental neighbors to immigrate to his British colony in 1682—Penns Woods, or Pennsylvania. By 1689, several thousand Germans had moved to Pennsylvania; by 1742, 100,000 had arrived— and by 1783, almost 300,000. Eventually, they would represent more than one third of America's population. It is easy to see that most Americans have at least some German blood flowing in their veins.

Although the Germans arrived in the seventeenth century, it wasn't until the early 1800's that their Christmas traditions took hold. Remember that they had precious little leisure time.

## LOUIS PRANG AND
## THE CHRISTMAS CARD

In the Prussian city of Breslau was born, in 1824, a frail child named Louis Prang, destined to become the king of Christmas cards. Early on, he fell in love with print design, wood and metal engraving, dyes, and color processing.

After working for a while in his brother's paper mill in Westphalia, he moved on to internships in the craft of printing throughout Europe. In 1848, fleeing the widespread social unrest on the Continent, Louis Prang eventually arrived in New York on April 5, 1850. Shortly thereafter, he moved to Boston, where, working for Frank Leslie, he became a master engraver, then a master lithographer.

By 1856 he was in business for himself, and in 1860 organized Prang & Company. By 1866 he had developed a technique he called "chromo" (lithographic copies of art), and was one of the first printers to use color—in fact, it was his use of color on business cards that set the stage for Christmas cards.

At the Vienna Exposition of 1873 Prang's life was changed by meeting Mrs. Arthur Ackerman, the wife of his agent in Britain. She had the foresight to suggest that he capitalize on a phenomenon that had begun in England during the 1840s, the Christmas card, and blitz London with dramatic multicolored cards.

Prang wasted no time: His vividly colored cards hit British shelves in time for the 1874 holiday season, and were snapped up by an entranced public. Earlier, in 1868, Prang had introduced illuminated chromos of Christmas scenes for hanging on American walls. By 1875 he expanded the idea from the walls to the mailbox of every American; his multicolored Christmas cards became the smash hit of the season. Each year that followed, he extended the line (including flowers, birds, butterflies, Nativity scenes, angels, winterscapes, elves, and Santa Claus). Inside were poetic lines penned by such literary luminaries as Longfellow, Whittier, and Bryant.

Production of these cards quickly soared into the millions. Ever since then, Christmas cards have helped to define our seasons.

So, in all your hauntings of flea markets, garage sales, bookstores, and antique stores, make a special effort to search out those lovely works of art: the cards and prints of Louis Prang. (I am deeply indebted to Peter E. Stevens's *The Mayflower Murderer and Other Forgotten Firsts in American History,* New York: William Morrow and Company, 1993, for this fascinating story.)

## THE CHRISTMAS SEASON

Anchoring the family Christmas festival was the Advent season. On the first Advent Sunday, four weeks before

Christmas, a large Advent wreath with a red candle would be hung. On each successive Advent Sunday another red candle would be added—and for each day, a paper star. On one side of each star was written an Old Testament verse, on the other side one from the New Testament; each day's verses were memorized by all the children in the family.

They also brought their counterpart of the Twelve Days of Christmas—only Germans, perhaps because their nights were longer, called them the Twelve Nights of Christmas. Shakespeare's *Twelfth Night* reflects the broad acceptance of the night aspect in Europe.

And while Germans might differ mightily over doctrine (most were either Lutheran or Catholic), they disagreed hardly at all on the Christmas traditions they loved.

In Germany, every year on December 6, St. Nicholas Day, a Christmarket, or fair, would be held. The towns would be filled with Christmas activities, with families flooding the narrow streets and buying cookies, candies, trees, and toys from booths along the way.

Christmas Eve for them was a deeply spiritual family time, a time to attend Christmas services, where they listened to music, the Gospel story, their children reciting verses from memory, etc. Everything possible that could be done to make it a children's festival was done.

Christmas was not a commercial season in those days, because they emphasized Christ and giving rather than self-gratification and excess.

According to Alfred Hottle's *1001 Christmas Facts and Fancies,* New York: A. T. De La Mare Co., 1938, December 24 has traditionally been such a family day in Germany that even restaurants are closed so everyone can be home. On Christmas Eve, after families return from church, Mother supervises the decoration of the tree, the setting up of the *Krippe* (Christmas crib), and perhaps even the installation of a musical holder for the Christmas tree. There are individual tables set up for each member of the family to complete the unfinished hand-made gifts such as "a soap rose, an artificial flower, a bit of lace, a sofa cushion, or an embroidered table spread." As for wrapping, the Germans revel in their own wrapping institution: *Julklapp.* Packages are wrapped in layers of *Julklapp* paper, each with a different person's name on it—only the last person named is entitled to the gift. And sometimes, after all the marathon unwrapping, there is no gift at all, merely directions for finding the gift! When all is ready, accompanied by the piano, all stream in to join hands and sing *"O Tannenbaum"* around the tree.

December 26 was considered a second Christmas (or "Little Christmas") and would be a time filled with talk, visiting neighbors and family, sleigh rides, games in house and barn, dances, and courtship. Outside, fences would be decorated with seasonal greenery, and on the door a Christmas wreath, crowned by a hunting horn.

## THE CHRISTMAS TREE

Germans brought the Christmas tree to America. Actually, use of the evergreen predated Christianity, in the Mithraic Festival of the Unconquerable Sun. When Christianity became the dominant Western religion, Church leaders decided to launch a countercelebration: a season centered on commemorating Christ's physical birth in Bethlehem and spiritual birth in the Jordan.

Evergreens have long been cherished because even in deep winter, when most plants and trees appear dead, they continue to evidence the continuity of life. Thus, it was natural that Christianity would seize upon it as a metaphor of the Trinity and eternal life. Early on, Pennsylvania Germans' evergreen of choice tended to be a juniper or cedar.

Martin Luther, seeking ways to make Christmas especially meaningful to his children, not only adopted the Nativity observances but also, popular legend has it, the Christmas tree. According to German tradition, wandering through the woods one serene Christmas Eve, Luther was filled with childlike wonder, gazing transfixed into the star-filled night. After a while, he cut down a small snow-flocked fir tree and set it up at home for his children. Since he could not bring the stars down, he substituted candles on the branches.

It was in the city of Strassburg, in 1604, that we have the first recorded use of the Christmas tree. However, both before then and after, it was not uncommon to bring fruit trees indoors in order to induce them to bloom during the Christmas season. Ever since 1604, the Christmas tree has been an integral part of German Christmas observance. When Prince Albert of Saxe-Coburg married Queen Victoria of England, he brought the Christmas-tree tradition with him.

So what did you do when there weren't any trees to be found—such as in the vast treeless steppes of Russia or the Great Plains of America? Where trees were scarce, their symbolic power was enhanced. People for miles around would journey to see the "Tannenbaum" (majestic evergreen) brought into the church from a distant forest. When such a tree was set up and decorated, children would gaze upon it with awe. Few indeed, in those treeless plains, ever experienced having a Christmas evergreen in their homes.

For Germans in forested America, the tree was an absolutely essential Christmas ingredient. "Bringing in the tree" was an annual tradition anticipated by the whole family. Inside homes there would most likely be not only a tree in the parlor, but one in each of the other downstairs rooms, as well as the bedrooms upstairs. These trees would be decorated (naturally, the family's main tree the most lavishly) with homemade strings of popcorn or cranberries, chains of brightly colored paper, gilded pinecones and locust seed pods, gold and rose ribbons, honesty plant, Queen Anne's lace, curly pretzels, dried apple rings, gilded nuts, shepherd crooks, and tiny baskets. Cookies of every shape imaginable, candy canes, and rich red apples hung on lower branches within easy range of children.

Decorating the tree was not far from mind all year long. Upstairs in the attic there would be trunks full of decorations and ornaments, most all hand-made and many generations old. On the branches would be molded red, blue, and saffron glass balls (many made in Germany) reflecting tiny points of light from the wax candles. These heirloom decorations, needless to say, were among the most cherished of all a family's possessions.

The tree was dedicated to the Christ Child and thus was taken very seriously. It was *not* a secular addition to the season. In fact, invariably—just to make sure no one lost sight of this truth—on the very top would be the Star, and just beneath it, the Christmas Angel.

## CHRISTMAS PUTZ

Another very appealing Germanic tradition is that of the *putz* (from the German verb *putzen,* signifying "to decorate or enhance in beauty." According to Pennsylvania Deutsch historians, "The American custom of erecting a putz seems to have originated with the Moravians but the custom long ago spread to non-Moravian households. Essentially, the putz is a landscape, built on the floor or on a table or portable platform. As a Christmas feature, it existed before the advent of Santa Claus or the American Christmas tree, and almost invariably had the creche as its focal point. The starting point for the construction was an irregular terrain of hills and valleys, covered with moss brought from the woods before a heavy frost and stored in a damp place. A mirror served as a lake, paths or roads were of sand or, in later years, colored sawdust. Evergreens' branches were converted into trees in scale with the rest of the putz or, if the whole creation was in miniature, ground pine, known locally as Jerusalem moss, made very convincing six-inch-tall trees. Driftwood, lichen-covered bark, and mossy stones from a brook were used for creating caves. Cardboard or wooden houses were set up as farmsteads or villages; human figures, in scale, went about their business of tilling fields or whatever the putz-maker chose to represent. A church putz would concentrate on background for the figures and appurtenances of the manger scene, of course" (*The Goschenhoppen Newsletter,* Green Lane, Pennsylvania, December 1985).

# CHRISTMAS FOOD!

While German cuisine needs no introduction, even so, at Christmas, cooks have traditionally outdone themselves. Christmas was announced by fragrances such as cinnamon, cloves, allspice, citron, lemon, ginger, mint, vanilla, and almond paste. Sandtart, springerlie, marzipan, lace, and ginger cookies would take form from heirloom tin cookie cutters. They took on the shapes of birds, rabbits, and other animals; beasts, fish, stars, angels; tulips, all sorts of flowers, and other shapes. Also, there would be stick-to-the-ribs mincemeat pies, *Kringel,* lebkuchen, fruitcake, glazed pound cake, pfeffernuss, and honey cake, as well as gingerbread men and animals that would end up on the windowsill. Combined, these fragrances repre-sented a time of year when body and soul communed in perfect harmony.

## CHRISTMAS EVE LEGENDS

One of the most intriguing traditions had to do with summer rainfall predictions. If you put out of doors three salted onion slices on Christmas Eve—representing the unpredictable growing months of June, July, and August—then invoked the blessing of the Trinity, on the morrow, when examining for moisture content, the dampest slice would foretell which month of the new year would be wettest. In some cases twelve (one for each month) would be put out.

There was also the belief that bread or water placed outside in the cold of Christmas Eve, by sunrise Christ Day would embody a special blessing, including magical curative powers.

Another tradition that children have loved has to do with farmyard animals, that, on this holy night, they are given special powers. It was believed that if a farmer went to his stable with his Bible and a lantern on this eve, and began reading the Bible at eight P.M. and continued until eleven P.M.—all the while eating a piece of bread with salt sprinkled on it—during the following hour he would be able to understand what the animals were saying. It was also believed that at precisely midnight Christmas Eve, the animals would kneel down in reverence.

## CHRISTMAS CAROLS

And what would Christmas be without such Germanic songs as *"O Tannenbaum,"* "Away in a Manger," Mendelssohn's

"Hark! The Herald Angels Sing," the fifteenth century's *"Est Ist Ein Ros"* ("Lo, How a Rose E'er Blooming"), and that ultimate Christmas carol *"Stille Nacht"* ("Silent Night")?

"Away in a Manger," although not technically a German hymn, has become part of this tradition. For better or worse, it seems, this carol will always be known as "Luther's Cradle Hymn." Since it was known that Martin Luther sang his children to sleep, it was therefore imagined (by someone long ago) that this lovely hymn could well have been the one he crooned.

The story of *"Stille Nacht"* has been told many times . . . but one of my favorites is that told by Father Richard, of the Old Santa Barbara Mission many years ago: "The organ of the little church of Arnsdorf near Salzburg, Austria, had in the last days before Christmas become unfit for further use. Mice had eaten at the bellows, and this seriously troubled the parish priest, Father Josef Mohr. He went to his organist and schoolmaster Franz Gruber and expressed his disappointment, saying, 'We must have something special for midnight mass.' "

Two days before Christmas in 1818, Father Mohr got the inspiration for a hymn from the beauty of the night. By Christmas Eve he had penned these now-familiar words to *"Stille Nacht"* ("Silent Night"):

## 1

*Stille Nacht, heilige Nacht!*
*Alles schläft, einsam wacht,*
*Nur das traute, hochheilige Paar,*

*Holder Knabe im lokkigem Haar.*

*Schlaf in himmlischer Ruh,*
*Schlaf in himmlischer Ruh.*

## 1

Silent night, holy night!
All is calm, all is bright,
Round yon virgin
  mother and Child,
Holy Infant, so tender
  and mild—
Sleep in heavenly peace,
Sleep in heavenly peace.

## 2

*Stille Nacht, heilige Nacht!*
*Hirten erst, kund gemacht,*

*Durch der Engel Halleluja,*

*Tönt es laut von fern und nah,*

*Christ, der Retter ist da,*

*Christ, der Retter ist da.*

## 2

Silent night, holy night!
Shepherds quake at the
  sight;
Glories stream from
  heaven afar,
Heavenly hosts sing
  alleluia—
Christ the Savior is
  born,
Christ the Savior is
  born!

| | |
|---|---|
| 3 | 3 |
| *Stille Nacht, heilige Nacht!* | Silent night, holy night! |
| *Gottes Sohn, O wie lacht,* | Son of God, love's pure light, |
| *Lieb aus deinem göttlichen Mund,* | Radiant beams from Thy holy face, |
| *Da uns schlägt die rettende Stund,* | With the dawn of redeeming grace— |
| *Christ in deiner Geburt,* | Jesus, Lord at Thy birth, |
| *Christ in deiner Geburt.* | Jesus, Lord at Thy birth. |

When Father Mohr showed his hymn to Franz Gruber, the organist caught the spirit of the words and captured them in the perfect tune. During midnight mass that Christmas Eve, the organ remained silent, but the congregation was not, as they sang this classic Christmas carol, accompanied by Gruber on the guitar.

## DER CHRISTKINDEL AND DER BELSNICKEL

For many years now I have wondered how one of America's cultural icons, Santa Claus, came to be. I was especially mystified about how such a secular figure could have evolved from such a Christlike churchman as St. Nicholas. And then I came across two of Germany's most significant contributions to Christmas: the *Christkindel* and the *Belsnickel,* both born in the Rhine valley and shadowed by the alpine heights where Germany, Switzerland, and France meet.

What especially intrigued me about these two Germanic figures is that they account for one of the most inexplicable qualities of Santa Claus—his omniscience, his Godlike ability to know everything about you: seeing you when you are awake or sleeping, knowing when you've "been bad or good." In short, possessing a power never attributed to St. Nicholas himself.

Both Catholic and Lutheran Germans brought *Christkindel* and *Belsnickel* across the Atlantic with them. Apparently, their long-ago ancestors felt St. Nicholas was an inadequate motivational figure for their children, hence they split him in two: on one side, the purity, innocence, and beauty of the Christ Child, known as *Christkindel* (also as Christ Kind, Christ Kindly, and later, as Kris Kringle); and, on the other, the dark, punishing, and rather demonic *Belsnickel,* who brought retribution and terror with him.

The role of *Christkindel* was generally given to a girl,

one who was attractive, blond, had a pleasing voice, could articulate well, and possessed an engaging sense of humor. In most cases, she would be dressed in white, with a red sash around her waist, a veil over her face, and a gold crown on her head; and she would carry a bundle of switches (or sticks). Usually she would be accompanied by an entourage of young girls (often arrayed in fantastic-looking costumes). A sack of nuts and candy would be carried by her or by one of her company. Her basket would contain toys. Sometimes the role of *Christkindel* would be played by a little girl (dressed entirely in white) who wore a golden crown and carried a small lighted Christmas tree in her hand.

Although the term *Christkindel* meant "Christ Child," it was a bit misleading, for in reality she was a hybrid of the Christ Child, a Christmas angel, and the ancient Germanic folk heroine (or good fairy) known as Hertha (sometimes Bertha, the hearth goddess, or the white lady, who guards German children). Early Germans would deck their homes with fir and evergreens to welcome her coming (during the winter solstice). Hertha's descent through the smoke to the hearthstones explains why our own Santa Claus descends through chimneys. In Germany, cakes are baked in the form of slippers; these slippers of Hertha are filled with small gifts so that Hertha, in return, will bestow on maidens and children the qualities of virtue, health, and beauty.

The *Christkindel,* later on Christmas Eve, supposedly would return when all were asleep and enter into the house through various openings, and would place the gifts on the table—*not* under a tree!—in the Christmas room. Although it was known that she came on donkeyback or muleback with great light around her, no one ever was privileged actually to see her make deliveries.

Inside the house, children would place empty plates on tables or windowsills, with the expectation that if they had been considered good, *der Christkindel* would leave them something special. If they had not, then they would get whatever *der Belsnickel* felt they deserved—most likely a chunk of coal.

On the stairs—as is done on the Day of the Wise Men, January 6, in many parts of the world—children would place their shoes, cleaned and polished, on Christmas Eve, hoping *der Christkindel* would fill them with nuts, candy, and that rarest of delicacies for nineteenth-century children: an orange. (Note here the substitution of shoes for Hertha's slippers.)

So angelic was the *Christkindel* that it is easy to see

why her visits were perceived as spiritual ones. The time varied, but usually it would be on Christmas Eve, after the lamps were lit, that one of the *Christkindel*'s companions would ring a bell in front of the window, then, after establishing contact with those inside, the question would be asked, "May the *Christkindel* come in?" Answered in the affirmative by the lady of the house, the entourage would enter, and almost immediately the *Christkindel* would begin grilling the children as to their behavior during the year.

Not surprisingly, children would often be frightened by all this commotion. They would be asked standard questions such as "Have you obeyed your parents all this year?" "Have you said your prayers every night?" If they had been good, they were rewarded with gifts; if they had been bad, they'd receive blows or be switched. Some *Christkindel*s would affect great doubt about the regularity of their prayer life, causing all the children to fall on their knees and recite them as proof of their assertions.

If there were children who had misbehaved—usually recalcitrant boys—a signal would be given that would summon *der Belsnickel*. Almost invariably—in the early days, at least, before degeneration set in—the two traveled together. *Der Belsnickel* would usually be a strong male with a deep booming bass voice. He would be covered by a shaggy fur coat (often with the fur worn on the inside); generally, he would either wear a grotesque mask or his face would be blackened with burnt cork. On his back would be a long chain that rattled terribly when he wished to frighten, and in one hand a bundle of switches. Oftentimes he'd wear patchwork clothes—anything well worn—and carry a large bow and a quiver of arrows. Attached to his long coattails would be bells. His stockings would be of green buckram, on his feet would be moccasins, around his ample waist a wide belt, and on his head would be an ancient hat worn low over his forehead. His old clothes would be ill fitting, so pillows often would exaggerate the already well-nourished figure. If he was beardless, he would most likely don an artificial beard; above it would be his trademark: a sinister upward-curving horned mustache.

He or an associate would carry a large feedsack—in which to stuff bad boys and carry them away—usually no farther than a snowbank in the vicinity, however. In another sack or basket would be the gifts for those who had been good.

Actually, *Belsnickel* is a corruption of what he had been called in Europe, *Pelznickel*. *Pelz* in German means "fur, or pelt," and *Nickel* is a shorter form of "St. Nicholas."

But there is a darker aspect as well, for the original meaning of *Nickel* also encompassed "fur demon," "fur imp," and a devillike character.

Unlike his gentler counterpart, *Belsnickel* rarely deigned to ask if he could come in . . . but stormed into the house like an avenging demon, rattling his chain, shaking his bells, and making fierce noises no one could understand. Bad boys would usually cringe in terror, but there was no refuge for them—custom dictated that even brothers or sisters would propel the erring ones forward to be punished with voice, switch, or lash.

In remote villages, *der Belsnickel* would sometimes attract the children by slamming open the front door. He would throw handfuls of nuts and candy on the floor, then, after children would scramble after his bait, pounce upon them, wielding whip and sticks right and left indiscriminately, on the basic premise that the unrighteous deserved it and the righteous weren't as righteous as people thought they were!

The secret of his omniscience was known to the adults, for he was in reality usually a neighbor, friend of the family, or close relative. Even "good" children shook to their core, wondering which of their hidden sins would be found out.

When he had stomped up the stairs into the parlor, there would be family waiting. Without any preliminaries, immediately the inquisition would commence:

"Have you said your bedtime prayers every night?"

"Have you memorized all your Sunday school verses?"

"Have you been naughty?"

"Did you faithfully do your chores every day?"

These were not merely general questions he asked: They got very specific and personal. And some of the *Belsnickels* would carry big black books with them, and inside would be written specific misdeeds that would be incorporated into the grilling:

"Did you or did you not, last October, deliberately let out of the corral Widow Schmidt's favorite milk cow, Old Bossy?"

"Weren't you the one who pushed over the outhouse two weeks ago, knowing full well the schoolmaster was in it?"

Or, for a child who professed good behavior:

"That won't do! Last year you promised not to sleep in church. And just last Sunday night you embarrassed your entire family by snoring. *By snoring!*"

He would often make them recite poetry or Bible verses they had learned for the Christmas program in the church.

When there was erring to be punished, *der Belsnickel* would lash out with his long switch—often making more noise than inflicting pain—or rap on the head, back, hand. After the grilling was over, he would toss down on the floor pieces of candy, nuts, or other goodies, and roar with laughter as the children fought one another for pieces.

As a matter of fact, through it all he laughed a lot. And it was funny—to the adults. Well, not always. Not when he severely reprimanded Father for failing to keep the harness well greased, or Mother for failing to keep the dishes clean or the furniture dust-free!

Once the serious part was done, *der Belsnickel* distributed his goodies: toys, oranges, apples, and candy. His job done at that house for the year, *Belsnickel* would often reveal who he was, and take refreshments.

Just as was true with the *Christkindel,* the *Belsnickel,* too, had another job to do that night, returning when all were asleep to punish the bad and reward the good. He it was who supposedly filled stocking legs, hats, caps, and the Christmas boxes that were set apart just for him.

In later years, as Americans became more secular and the old traditions lost their force, belsnickeling became merely a form of Christmas roistering. More masks were sold at Christmas than at Halloween, as gangs would flood the more urban areas with hilarity. Many would perform music, with and without instruments, "mumming" at each door for treats. On Christmas Eve, the streets would be filled with revelers out for fun and mischief, costumed as bandit chiefs, Indians, clowns, harlequins, devils, demons, ragamuffins, and performers, making the night hideous with kettledrums, trumpets, pennywhistles, cornets, violins, bones, tambourines—many having had far too much to drink. Modern mummers parades, such as Philadelphia's, maintain this tradition.

But . . . before the traditions had degenerated, they filled a very special role in American life. In truth, they complemented each other well: beauty and the beast, the angelic and the demonic, the love of the Christ Child and the spirit of the law in the New Testament, and the awesomeness of the Lord and the letter of the law in the Old Testament.

Perhaps the finest summation of these complementary roles is found in Fritz Williams's *Der Belsnickel* (*Aprise*, December 1988):

"Gruff and mean as he was, the *Belsnickel* called attention to the dark side of life—selfishness, evil, and torment. He represented the terror of being known through and through down to the tiniest secret, the awful possibility of evil claiming its own. But then, in contrast to the *Belsnickel,* his rough and surly conduct, the unmerited goodness and generosity of the *Christkindel* seemed all the more beautiful and miraculous."

While the Teutonic Germans may not have worn their hearts on their sleeves, this most certainly does not mean they were not a caring people. For instance, while variations were freely permitted, undergirding their Christmas traditions were certain nonnegotiables. Paramount was this: No one could refuse *der Belsnickel*'s rewards or punishments—regardless of how young or how old you might be. Because of this unwritten code, *Belsnickel*s were able to double as angels of mercy and deliverance. When a family was suffering financially, with hardly anything to wear or eat, the neighbors were able secretly to come to their aid through gifts the *Belsnickel* would leave behind. Pride was preserved and no one lost face.

The institution of *der Christkindel/der Belsnickel* survived for about 150 years in America before being swallowed by that department store import, Santa Claus. In a later volume we will explore his fascinating evolution through St. Nicholas, the *Christkindel,* the *Belsnickel,* Moore's "Visit of St. Nicholas," Christmas cards, and Thomas Nast's famous cartoons in *Harper's Illustrated Weekly* magazines.

Today, in turn-of-the-millennium society, there is an almost frantic search for bedrock upon which to build a life. The media has, by and large, shown itself to be almost devoid of interest in Judeo-Christian values; the same applies to advertisers.

That is why there is a turning back to what we once had. We could do far worse than to return to the Germanic Christmas traditions chronicled in this introduction. Doing so might revitalize our Christmas seasons. Do *you* think it's worth a try?

## THE FOURTH COLLECTION

Of the eleven stories in this forth collection, three of the authors you will remember as a result of their inclusion in earlier collections: Pearl S. Buck ("Stranger, Come Home"), Temple Bailey ("Candle in the Forest" and "The Locking in of Lisabeth"), and Hartley F. Dailey ("The Red

Mittens" and "Yet Not One of Them Shall Fall"). Of the other eight stories, other than my own, Fulton Oursler's "A String of Blue Beads" has gradually become almost a Christmas icon, "Bethany's Christmas Carol" is one of the most sentimental of all Christmas stories, Cathy Miller's "Delayed Delivery" has experienced a meteoric rise in popularity during its first seven years of life, "The Tallest Angel" is a powerful story deserving to be heard every Christmas, Fritz Vincken's "Truce in the Forest" is one of the most moving stories to come out of World War II, "Pink Angel" reminds us of just how hollow achievement is without loved ones to notice it, and Bill Vaughan's "Tell Me a Story of Christmas" is unique in that while it is one of the shortest Christmas stories ever written, it also is one that manages to encapsulate *all* of them.

## CODA

Virtually every day's mail brings welcome correspondence from you. Many of your letters are testimonials to the power of certain stories; virtually *all* of them express gratitude for the series. Others include favorite stories for possible inclusion down the line (some of them Christmas-related and others tying in with other genre collections we are working on). These letters from you not only brighten each day for us—but they help to provide the stories which make possible future story anthologies.

May the good Lord bless and guide each of you.

You may contact me at the following address:

Joe Wheeler, Ph.D.
c/o Doubleday Religion Department
1540 Broadway
New York, New York 10036

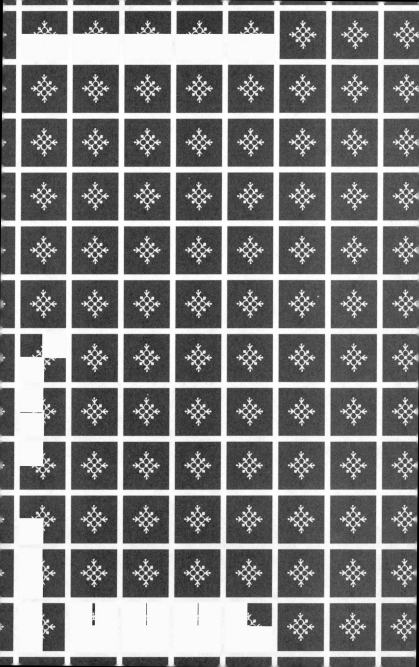

# A String of Blue Beads

✦

## FULTON OURSLER

*One of the loveliest and most beloved of all Christmas short stories was penned by Fulton Oursler. Oursler's story reminds us that possessions without someone to share them with are hollow and meaningless. He also reminds us once again that one can't pay more than "all one has" for a gift.*

*(Charles) Fulton Oursler cast a*

*giant shadow over his time (1893–1952). Besides editing* Metropolitan, Liberty, Cosmopolitan, *and* Reader's Digest, *he was a prolific writer of short stories, screenplays, and books, perhaps best known for his* The Greatest Story Ever Told.

Pete Richards was the loneliest man in town on the day Jean Grace opened his door. You may have seen something in the newspapers about the incident at the time it happened, although neither his name nor hers was published, nor was the full story told as I tell it here.

Pete's shop had come down to him from his grandfather. The little front window was strewn with a disarray of old-fashioned things: bracelets and lockets worn in days before the Civil War, gold rings and silver boxes, images of jade and ivory, porcelain figurines.

On this winter's afternoon a child was standing there, her forehead against the glass, earnest and enormous eyes studying each discarded treasure, as if she were looking for something quite special. Finally she straightened up with a satisfied air and entered the store.

The shadowy interior of Pete Richards's establishment was even more cluttered than his show window. Shelves were stacked with jewel caskets, dueling pistols, clocks and lamps, and the floor was heaped with andirons and mandolins and things hard to find a name for.

Behind the counter stood Pete himself, a man not more than thirty but with hair already turning gray. There was a bleak air about him as he looked at the small customer who flattened her ungloved hands on the counter.

"Mister," she began, "would you please let me look at that string of blue beads in the window?"

Pete parted the draperies and lifted out a necklace. The turquoise stones gleamed brightly against the pallor of his palm as he spread the ornament before her.

"They're just perfect," said the child entirely to herself. "Will you wrap them up pretty for me, please?"

Pete studied her with a stony air. "Are you buying these for someone?"

"They're for my big sister. She takes care of me. You see, this will be the first Christmas since Mother died. I've been looking for the most wonderful Christmas present for my sister."

"How much money do you have?" asked Pete warily.

She had been busily untying the knots in a handkerchief and now she poured out a handful of pennies on the counter.

"I emptied my bank," she explained simply.

Pete Richards looked at her thoughtfully. Then he carefully drew back the necklace. The price tag was visible to him but not to her. How could he tell her? The trusting look of her blue eyes smote him like the pain of an old wound.

"Just a minute," he said, and turned toward the back of the store. Over his shoulder he called, "What's your name?" He was very busy about something.

"Jean Grace."

When Pete returned to where Jean Grace waited, a package lay in his hand, wrapped in scarlet paper and tied with a bow of green ribbon. "There you are," he said shortly. "Don't lose it on the way home."

She smiled happily at him over her shoulder as she ran out the door. Through the window he watched her go, while desolation flooded his thoughts. Something about Jean Grace and her string of beads had stirred him to the depths of a grief that would not stay buried. The child's hair was wheat yellow, her eyes sea blue, and once upon a time, not long before, Pete had been in love with a girl with hair of that same yellow and with eyes just as blue. And the turquoise necklace was to have been hers.

But there had come a rainy night—a truck skidding on a slippery road—and the life was crushed out of his dream.

Since then Pete Richards had lived too much with his grief in solitude. He was politely attentive to customers, but after business hours his world seemed irrevocably empty. He was trying to forget in a self-pitying haze that deepened day by day.

The blue eyes of Jean Grace jolted him into acute remembrance of what he had lost. The pain of it made him recoil from the exuberance of holiday shoppers. During the next ten days trade was brisk; chattering women swarmed in, fingering trinkets, trying to bargain. When the last customer had gone, late on Christmas Eve, he sighed with relief. It was over for another year. But for Pete Richards the night was not quite over.

The door opened and a young woman hurried in. With an inexplicable start, he realized that she looked familiar, yet he could not remember when or where he had seen her before. Her hair was golden yellow and her large eyes were blue. Without speaking, she drew from her purse a package loosely unwrapped in its red paper, a bow of green ribbon with it. Presently, the string of blue beads lay gleaming again before him.

"Did this come from your shop?" she asked.

Pete raised his eyes to hers and answered softly, "Yes, it did."

"Are the stones real?"

"Yes. Not the finest quality—but real."

"Can you remember who it was you sold them to?"

"She was a small girl. Her name was Jean. She bought them for her older sister's Christmas present."

"How much are they worth?"

"The price," he told her solemnly, "is always a confidential matter between the seller and the customer."

"But Jean has never had more than a few pennies of spending money. How could she pay for them?"

Pete was folding the gay paper back into its creases, rewrapping the little package just as neatly as before.

"She paid the biggest price anyone can ever pay," he said. "She gave all she had."

There was a silence then that filled the little curio shop. He saw the faraway steeple; a bell began ringing. The sound of the distant chiming, the little package lying on the counter, the question in the eyes of the girl, and the strange feeling of renewal struggling unreasonably in the heart of the man—all had come to be because of the love of a child.

"But why did you do it?"

He held out the gift in his hand.

"It's already Christmas morning," he said. "And it's my misfortune that I have no one to give anything to. Will you let me see you home and wish you a Merry Christmas at your door?"

And so, to the sound of many bells and in the midst of happy people, Pete Richards and a girl whose name he had yet to hear, walked out into the beginning of the great day that brings hope into the world for us all.

# Bethany's Christmas Carol

## MABEL MCKEE

*This story has long been one of my family's favorites. It depicts how little it avails if one has wealth without personal caring. Also, that much "illness" is in reality the result of wounds to the spirit. Equally important, it exemplifies how important it is that nurses genuinely care for and love their patients.*

*Mabel McKee, early in the twen-*

*tieth century, was responsible for some of the most memorable inspi-*
*rational literature in print. Sadly, little is known of her today.*

They called her Carol Meloney eleven months of the year at Bethany Hospital. But during the twelfth, which was December, they termed her "Christmas Carol," and she was so merry and happy that most of the patients there thought that was the sole reason the dusky-eyed, auburn-haired little nurse was called a Christmas name.

But the head of the nurses and all the others down to the newest probationer could have told you that the reason was that Carol was born on Christmas Day just twenty-one years before! Also that her frail little mother, who had seen five little brothers and sisters come into the parsonage home before Carol, declared that her newest baby sang instead of cried on that Christmas Day she was born, and had said to her minister husband, "Let's call her Carol, dear."

Always in that parsonage home, from which the

mother soon slipped away, they called her "Carol, dear," and she was as fragrant and sweet and lovely as a Christmas carol.

But this Christmas week, Carol wasn't happy, didn't want to sing. Down in the baby ward lay her wee namesake, until a week ago snuggled beside its little mother. But that little mother had, without warning, slipped away, leaving her precious baby to the happy nurse of Bethany whose name she had given it because she wanted the baby to be merry and cheerful and lovable too—had slipped away without breaking her silence or letting anybody there know who were her relatives, if she had any, or if there were some other persons with a claim on the child. Carol lifted the little one in her arms and said, "I'm going to keep her in my own family. The mother really gave her to me, you know. There is my oldest sister, Marie, both of whose babies died a year ago. I'm going to ask Marie to keep her because she is another Christmas Carol."

Standing there close beside the tiny basket bed, Carol had made all her plans. She would go home to Marie on Christmas Day, and she would lay the baby in her arms and say, "I've brought you another Christmas Carol, dear, whose mother has slipped away just as mine did while I was still a babe."

Marie *couldn't* refuse to keep the baby, and the child would take the lonely ache out of Marie's heart. Oh, this Christmas promised to be the very happiest one she had known, just because she had such a wonderful gift to give. But "best-laid schemes o' mice and men gang aft a-gley." Young Dr. Greig assigned her to the peritonitis case in Room 26 when the regular nurse came down with the measles. The patient refused to change nurses again, and since she was really quite ill, no one dared offend her. Carol looked down at the white toes of her oxfords when the superintendent told her that she would have to change her plans about going home for Christmas, and then the tears came in spite of her best efforts.

"Oh, I'm not thinking of myself," the girl sobbed, "but if Marie doesn't get my blessed baby as a Christmas present, I'm afraid she'll not have such a happy holiday."

The head nurse patted Carol's red-brown curls. "Patient in twenty-six is sick at heart as well as in body," she confided. "We assigned you to the case because we thought that you could cheer her up. She and her husband have been drawing apart for a long time. She is grieving, and it's your duty to try to coax bitterness from her heart and smiles back to her lips."

Carol found Mrs. Joseph Cartwright an ideal patient in spite of what people said about her being a bit strange. When her friends sent her great boxes of flowers, she always divided them with some patients who had none. She introduced the young nurse to the club women who came to see her, and in every way treated her with such consideration that at times she felt like a sister to the rich woman.

But when everybody was gone, Mrs. Cartwright just turned her face toward the wall and lay very still, speaking to Carol only when she wanted something. She even protested when the girl brought in two holly wreaths for the windows. "I do not celebrate Christmas anymore, my dear," she explained. "Take the wreaths to someone who can share the Christmas spirit."

On this morning before Christmas Day she seemed more nervous than usual, and the doctor took Carol outside the room. "Don't let her have visitors today," he warned. "They will only make her remember other holidays which have been happier. We must keep her from doing much of that, or she will have a relapse."

Carol was almost ready to go shopping then. Her eyes held a glint of happy anticipation. All her presents for her own people had been sent home, but she had to get an array of gifts for tiny Carol. The other nurses at Bethany wanted to help make the orphan baby's first Christmas a real one.

She found the best substitute in the hospital for her patient, and then started on her way upstairs, to her own room. She heard the choir next door practicing Christmas carols. They would sing them that evening in the hospital, winding through the corridors and stopping at the doors of patients who were convalescing.

Carol listened. *"Away in a manger,"* they began, and immediately she thought of the tiny baby which was now hers, lying in its plain little basket in the baby ward, and though she had a dozen things to do, the girl ran through the garlanded halls, down the stairs to the floor below, and into the baby's room, where she lifted her wee namesake and held her close in her arms.

"Marie's darling baby!" she whispered. "You're going to make our Marie happy again and drive away the sad shadows from her eyes. You little precious!"

The tiny baby was beautiful, with tiny petallike hands, cupid's-bow mouth, and hair that was going to be golden. She was dressed in a little white slip of the regulation hospital style. Carol was to get her a beautiful nainsook dress, delicately embroidered, with the money the other nurses had given. Oh, how hard it was for her to wait until she could get to town and select it!

Back into the gay corridors she skipped, and down the stairs just in time to meet a messenger boy with a package for her patient. It bore the seal of the city's most expensive jewelry shop. When the boy seemed bewildered, Carol offered to take it to Mrs. Cartwright.

Perhaps that is all she would have known about the jeweler's box had not the substitute asked her to stay a moment while she made a telephone call, and Carol stayed, straightening a magazine here or a bottle there as she waited.

The gleam of platinum caught her attention. The package had been unwrapped and disclosed a beautiful white satin box in which was an expensive wristwatch, a wreath with diamonds surrounding the face. Mrs. Cartwright's hand held the white card on which were the words "Christmas greetings," and the gray one under it which bore, in engraved letters, "Joseph Cartwright."

For one minute she studied the cards and the gift, then snapped the white velvet box shut and laid it on the table beside her bed. Tears trickled from under her closed eyelids.

Carol had seen it all through the big mirror, even the two cards that carried no hint of the affection that changes gifts from cold, inanimate *things* to love tokens.

"Oh, the poor dear!" she sighed. "Why couldn't he have just said 'with love'?"

The substitute nurse came back, and Carol hurried out into the spicy cold—hurried by all the late shoppers with their odd-shaped parcels, past people who smiled and called "Merry Christmas" to each other through the falling snow, and as she hurried she sang softly to herself.

At the corner she decided to carry a great bowl of holly into Mrs. Cartwright's room that evening. At the next one she decided to carry tiny Carol into that room the next morning and see if the little Christmas visitor couldn't change that tired, heartbroken look into a tender smile. At the third corner she decided to buy Mrs. Cartwright a gift and write on the card "With love— Carol."

At the big store where she bought tiny Carol's Christmas dress, little wool shirts and stockings, and a pink and white woolly baby blanket, she went on the quest for a gift for the sick lady. She didn't have much to spend. All the brothers and sisters and nieces and nephews had sadly depleted her purse. And wee Carol had almost finished it. She never dreamed that babies were such expensive bits of joy.

She wandered to the book counter. She thought of a gift book, full of sentiment, and with a beautiful binding. The head of the department came to wait on her. Carol liked the "head," for she loved books as she did people, and talked of them as if they were alive.

"I'm buying a little book for Mrs. Joseph Cartwright," she confided. "Do you know her?"

"Know her? I should said I do. Why, she used to bring her little son in here for me to help her choose his nursery rhyme books. She was the most adorable mother I ever knew."

"Oh." Carol's eyes opened wide. "I didn't know she had a little boy. She never mentions him. She's ill at Bethany Hospital, and I am her nurse."

The other woman's hands clasped Carol's. "Didn't you know she had a little boy? He died about three years ago? Haven't you ever heard what a bitter tragedy her home life has become?"

Then Carol felt more than pity for her patient—felt understanding and real love. Meanwhile the girl was talking—telling of Mrs. Cartwright's generous gifts to orphanages, to charity institutions, to every place that held a needy child.

Swayed by a new feeling, Carol bought the most beautiful book in the department and a dainty Christmas card, which read:

> *I'm giving myself instead of wealth,*
> *And all I have to you.*

She knew, somehow, that Mrs. Cartwright would really know she meant it. Hugging the bundles in her arms, she went out into the snow, to be pelted on the way home with snowballs by two little boys, to race down the avenue with other late Christmas shoppers, and tell everybody who passed her, "Merry Christmas."

She had forgotten the disappointment she had felt because she couldn't be with her family. She was thinking of Christmas now as a day to especially love and be especially interested in the whole wide, weary world.

As she passed the tiny chapel on the corner, she slipped in to see the beautiful decorations. Just above the chancel hung a painting of the Christ as a tiny babe in the rude Bethlehem manger, and underneath it was the inscription:

*He gave the world's greatest Gift to all.*

It was right then the beautiful Christmas idea was born in her heart. It came with a cruel twist, though it was beautiful. She *couldn't* do it, she told herself. She would be robbing not only herself, but Marie, whom she loved so dearly. For she knew the little baby would bring joy to Marie through all the years that followed.

*But Marie can love another baby,* the voice said. *Hasn't she often talked of adopting one? All you need to do is to encourage her, and she'll go right to an orphanage and get one.*

Carol clasped her hands in front of her and knelt and prayed. Was it right for her to give away the wee baby for whom the mother had given her life? Would it bring joy to Mrs. Cartwright's heart? Would she accept the gift even if it were offered?

*You can offer it,* the voice whispered. *You can try to bring her great joy.* Carol bowed her head still lower.

Lovingly, she held close to her heart the miniature nainsook dress she had bought for her tiny namesake. And as she held it, there came to her mind the message her mother had left for her when she slipped away a few weeks after her birth: "I'm giving you to your sisters, dear baby, so they will not miss me so much. Babies heal heartaches better than anything else can. You were my Christmas gift, so I know you will be a love baby and love girl and then a love woman, who will love others all through your life."

Marie had told her that many, many times when she had been naughty and selfish in her childhood—told her that she must never cause anything except happiness, because she was a Christmas Carol to sing through the years.

Carol held the tiny dress closer and looked at the picture. "I'll give it for your sake, Jesus." Back in her room again, she unpacked the little bundles, laid the nainsook dress and Christmas card close together, then slipped up to Mrs. Cartwright's room. The patient had had her supper, the substitute said, and did not wish to be disturbed.

Carol went to the baby ward next, took tiny Carol back to her room, dressed her in the nainsook dress, and wrapped her in the pink and white blanket. Then she carried her to Mrs. Cartwright's room, entered softly on tiptoe, laid the tiny mite in the curve of her patient's arm, put the card in her hand, then slipped out before the sick woman could turn her head.

Carol's bell rang sharply half an hour later. Breathlessly, she answered the call. Mrs. Cartwright's curved arm still held the baby. Her mouth was smiling though her eyes were misty.

"Oh, my dear, my dear," she began, "how could you be so generous as to give the tiny Christmas Carol you had planned to take to your sister? Oh, the wonder of your gift!" (The substitute only that afternoon had told Mrs. Cartwright the story of the tiny baby which Carol loved so dearly.) She was going to keep the baby. She wanted to adopt it, and wished a message sent asking Mr. Cartwright to come at once.

He always wanted me to take a baby into our home," she whispered to Carol, "but until you gave me little Carol, I felt I couldn't hold one in my arms after Billy died."

Half an hour later Carol heard a rush outside the door, and saw a big man, whom she instantly knew as Mr. Cartwright, coming into the room. This time she fairly ran out into the hall, where she felt herself the most lonely person in the whole world. She wandered on until she reached the corridor, where the choir from the nearby church and nurses off duty were forming in line, ready for their march through the hospital. She heard the "specials" gently opening doors so their patients would not miss the singing.

She slipped into the line, right after the probationer whose mother had died a few weeks before, and patted the girl's shoulder comfortingly and held her hand as they began to march. Her other hand held one of the open songbooks, and her sweet, girlish soprano sang with the others.

They passed the men's ward, and the old veteran, whose Grand Army button shone as did his eyes, waved his hand at them; passed the women's ward, where there was a little lame girl keeping time to the music with her crutch, passed many other rooms, and entered the corridor off of which opened the room Carol had just left.

She glanced through the door ajar. Mrs. Cartwright still held the baby close to her heart, and her hand was resting on the bowed head of her husband. Her eyes were so beautiful and brilliant that Carol knew the spirit of Christmas was in her heart at last.

# *Joey's Miracle*

## HARTLEY F. DAILEY

"Miracles just don't happen anymore." But six-year-old Joey didn't believe that for a minute—he was sure God would bring him a bicycle. With the Depression raising fiscal havoc, and most people struggling just to find food for the table, clearly the little boy was setting himself up for certain disappointment.

Hartley Dailey, author of the

*beloved Christmas classic "The Red Mittens," still lives and writes from the hills of his native Springfield, Ohio.*

They say the age of miracles is past. They say the prophets are all dead, that shining angels no longer fly down from the realm above, bringing divine messages to mortal men, handing out rewards to the good and punishment to the guilty. All of which is true, of course. One seldom meets a prophet these days, and angels are a remarkably scarce commodity, even in storybooks.

But neither prophets nor angels are absolutely essential to a miracle. Rewards—or punishments—may come at the hands of the most unlikely individuals, and the most mundane of gifts may waken wonder in the eyes of a small boy. Let me tell you the story of Joey's bicycle.

It happened in the depths of the great Depression of the thirties. I had come up from the hills to find a good steady job in the city. There I met Betty, and we fell in love and were married. Soon we bought a nice house in a good neighborhood and settled down for life, or so we thought. But you know the saying about the best laid plans of mice and men. Came the Depression and I lost my job. We were faced with house payments, a family to feed and clothe, and very little money in the bank. Like many others, I could see very little hope of any better times in the near future.

Now it so happened I had a little farm back in the hills, which I had inherited from my grandfather. Many times, over the years, friends had urged me to sell it, to invest the money, or use it to help pay for my city place. But I had stubbornly held on to it, partly because it made a nice vacation retreat, and partly because I loved the old place, the first home I had ever known.

So at this juncture, faced with the prospect of losing everything we owned, we decided to cut our losses and get out while we still had something left. We sold our home for just enough to pay off the mortgage, a sizable loss, but we were fortunate to get off so lightly. At least we still had a home back in the hills, not much, it is true, but free and clear of any encumbrance. We had forty acres on which to raise our food, at least. We were better off than thousands of others. So on a clear spring morning we set off, all our possessions following in a truck, to make our home in a little cabin in the hills.

Over the months, due to doctor's bills, taxes, and other unavoidable expenses, our savings slowly dwindled. I had bought a couple of cows, some chickens, and some pigs, and we managed to raise enough food for our own use, plus a little to sell. But of course, prices were very low, and after all, how much can one raise on forty hilly acres?

We were facing our second Christmas on the farm, and prospects were very poor. Our older children, David, twelve, and Melissa, ten, were old enough to understand our poverty. They could accept the fact of having only an extra good dinner, plus maybe some warm socks or mittens, for Christmas. But Joey was six, and Joey wanted a bicycle. Useless to explain to him that bicycles cost a lot of money, and only rich little boys could have such luxuries. He was firmly convinced Santa Claus would bring him one. No use, either, to tell him Santa Claus didn't come to see poor little boys. Santa Claus had been to see him before, and he didn't understand the difference. With the help of his sister, he wrote a letter to the old saint and gave it to me to mail.

Sometime later, his friends at school must have cast some doubt on the power, or maybe even the existence, of Santa Claus. Or perhaps he simply decided to take his problem to a higher power. At any rate, he came to me one evening as I read the paper after the chores were done.

"I'm sure I'll get my bicycle now, Dad," he said.

"Why is that?" I asked absently.

" 'Cause Johnny said, 'If you pray to God, you're sure to get your wish!' " Johnny was his best school friend. "And that's just what I'm gonna do," he concluded.

"Oh, Joey, Joey." I took him in my arms. "Don't you know God can't grant every wish we make? What if there's some other little boy, one who needs a bike much worse than you do? Wouldn't God have to grant his wish instead?"

He wasn't convinced. "I don't know about needs," he said confidently, "but I'm sure God could never find a boy who *wants* one more."

So things stood on Saturday, just a week before Christmas. Joey still included a plea for his bicycle every time he said his prayers. And he went around with such a cheerful smile, as though the coveted property were already on the back porch. He was so good, he was almost insufferable.

We had saved up a whole crate of eggs, which I intended to sell in the city, as well as a considerable quantity of turnips, a few apples, and a few potatoes we thought we could spare. On that Saturday morning I set out for the city, determined to sell my produce to the greatest advantage, and get what little Christmas I could for everyone. Joey had wanted to go along, but I wouldn't permit it, for the weather was bitter cold, and it was a long trip. Besides, I expected to spend a lot of time walking the streets. It would be too much for a six-year-old. Later, I was glad I hadn't brought him.

It was about three o'clock in the afternoon when I had finally sold my produce, and such shopping as I could afford was done. I had parked my car and walked over much of the business section, since I had a trailer and couldn't park it easily. I was cold, bone-weary, and my feet were soaking wet from walking in the snow. Because of this, I took a shortcut through the alley, past the police station. Thus it was that I came upon the auction.

The police department employees, as they do periodically, were auctioning off an accumulation of unclaimed articles. Already, when I came on the scene, they had sold a surprising miscellany of lost, abandoned, or confiscated items: two old cars, guns, bicycles, luggage, clothing, even one sad-looking, half-frozen hound dog.

The last item of the day was on the block, a little boy's sixteen-inch bicycle. It was a sad little wreck, its paint all gone, its fenders bent, one tire flat, and the handlebars drooping. Still, with a little paint, a little hammer and wrench work, and with that tire patched, how different it would look! Trouble was, after such little Christmas shopping as I had done, and buying enough gasoline to get me back home, I had only a single half dollar in my pocket.

The auctioneer, a big, paunchy, red-faced police sergeant, was calling desperately for bids. In vain he called for five dollars, two dollars—one. Nobody seemed interested. Finally, just as he seemed on the point of losing his voice completely, he stopped shouting, looked over the crowd in a kind of exasperated way, then said in a voice half pleading, half threatening, "Please, for heaven's sake, won't somebody give me a bid, just *any* bid—but get it started."

That half dollar burned like a red-hot coal in my pocket. Should I try it? It was ridiculous, of course. Start it that low, and somebody was sure to top my bid. And I didn't have any more money, not a single penny, to bid any higher. But I had to do it.

"Fifty cents," I called out.

*Bang* went the gavel.

"Mister," said the old sergeant, "you've bought a bicycle." I've had a soft place in my heart for big, red-faced policemen ever since.

Some fellow in the crowd started to protest, saying he hadn't been given a chance to bid before it sold. He didn't like such high-handed tactics, and he was making no bones about it. The sergeant turned on him with a baleful scowl.

"True," he stormed, "you wasn't. And where was you, may I ask, when I was standin' here screamin' myself hoarse just to get an openin' bid? It's cold in this here shed, an' I been standin' here all afternoon just tryin' to coax another nickel out of you tightwads. It's near my quittin' time, an' I got a lot of work to do yet, writin' up the records of these sales. I'm quittin' here an' now. This gentleman bought the bike, an' there's an end to it!"

I took my purchase away, loaded it in my trailer, and covered it with the sacks in which I had hauled my turnips to town. Christmas Day, its tire patched, its fenders and handlebars straightened, and with a bright new coat of paint, it stood beneath our Christmas tree. And if that old sergeant could have seen the joy on the face of one little boy, I'm sure he would have been glad for all the cold and hoarseness he suffered over it.

Joey took it all very much for granted. "See, Daddy," he told me very confidently, "God didn't find another little boy who needed a bike more than me. Or at least not one who *wanted* it more," he added.

That bicycle proved to be of much better stuff than its first appearance indicated. Joey rode it up hill and down dale till he had quite outgrown it. In fact, you can still see it hanging from a couple of pegs on my garage wall, and it still looks better than it did the day I bought it.

Of course, Joey is a grown man now, with a little Joey of his own. Over six feet two, he is a big, strapping fellow who did his stint in the marines, during the Korean War, and came home to fill a much better job than his daddy ever had. A hard-headed, intensely practical individual, you would say, with no nonsense about him. But if ever you should meet him, don't tell him the age of miracles is past. He'd never believe you.

# And It Was Christmas Morning

✦

## TEMPLE BAILEY

*Priorities. Each life is built on them, consists of their varied order. Always has, always will. In this old story, two women within the same extended family prioritize their family relationships differently—at least they did before a certain Christmas Eve.*

*This is a* wonderful *story, one that moves me deeply every time I read it. It is, I submit, one of the greatest Christmas stories ever written. I have been saving it for this special fourth collection.*

*Only recently did I discover, for the first time, the complete text.*

*Temple Bailey (1880's?–1953) was one of the most popular and highest-paid authors in the world during the first three decades of the twentieth century, writing not only hundreds of short stories but a number of best-selling novels.*

*To learn more about barn animals in Christmas Eve legendry, see the introduction to this volume.*

Christmas was a week away, and everything was ready.

"Isn't it joyful, Peter," said Peter's mother.

"Yes." Peter's voice lacked enthusiasm. "And now let's talk."

"But, my darling, I haven't time. I must telephone Mrs. Maddox about the old ladies from the home who are going to dine with us Christmas Day, and I must talk over my menus with Martha. And Daddy will be here before we know it."

"Well," said Peter resignedly, and got out his Noah's Ark, and set the animals all in a row on the rug in front of the fire.

The rug was a velvety, deep-piled thing with honey-colored lights. Peter liked to think of it as the sands of the desert. When the animals walked on it, two by two, the camels and leopards and all the lions, the effect was tremendous. Peter was, of course, too old for Noah's Ark. He was seven and he went to school. But he loved his Noah's Ark in the same way that he loved the great log in the fire, and the sound of the wind booming about the high and handsome apartment house in which he lived, and in the same way that he liked the shine of the candles in the dining room and the smell of the roast meat for dinner.

His mother sat at the telephone and told Mrs. Maddox things in the same words that she had told them to Peter.

"Isn't it joyful, Maude? I have everything ready except wrapping the parcels, and Peter is going to help me with that on Saturday. We are tying them with blue, sprinkled with silver stars. We are so tired of red. And the blue gives a hint of the Madonna idea. Yes? Oh, there will be ten of us—we three, and the two old ladies from the home, and Big Peter's brother, Robert, and his wife and three boys. No, we are not going to have a tree."

Peter pricked up his ears. His mother hadn't told him that. No tree. No thick, spicy fragrance of pine, no spiny branches that grew brittle as the days went on and strewed the waxed floor with needles like the ground in the forest.

"Mother," he said as she hung up the receiver, "why didn't you tell me that there won't be any tree?"

"Oh, did you hear? Well, you've always had a tree and I thought of something new. It's a secret."

"I don't want a secret." Peter's eyes were stormy. "I want a tree."

"But, darling . . ."

Peter knew that tone. His mother's logic would be convincing. They never quarreled. Peter had had it impressed upon him that quarreling wasn't well bred. His polite protests always ended in acquiescence. He was not in the least afraid of his mother, not physically afraid. But he grew so tired of her eternal rightness. Although he wouldn't have called it that. There never seemed to be any room for your own ideas.

So he dropped the subject and set three camels out alone on the honey-colored rug. Martha, the cook, had come into the dining room, which was just beyond the library, and was talking to his mother. There was second maid, Lulu, setting the table, and she stopped and listened to his mother's instructions.

"I am making my lists up, Martha, so that you can put in your orders early."

She read the menus, and Peter, traveling with his camels over the sandy desert on a magical quest, was aware of an appetizing succession of foods, from which he mentally picked out his favorites—candied sweet potatoes and Marie-Louise soup. He liked the name of that soup so much that he had always eaten it in spite of its rather complicated flavor. His father had shown him a picture of Marie-Louise.

"If you have any suggestions, Martha, let me know now. The color scheme will be green and white. I'll order the centerpiece from the florist, Lulu; there'll be mistletoe for the big silver bowl, and tall white candles. And the canapes must be green, Martha, and pistachio ice cream in Christmas-tree forms . . ."

The drowsily listening Peter was aware of the cut-and-driedness of it all. They had turkey every other Sunday in winter, and canapes and ice cream were no novelties. He didn't know what he wanted. But there was a picture in a book of a pudding all in flames. And his father had read to him about the Cratchits and of how *their* pudding bobbed in the copper. His mother's bright voice stopped. Martha went back to the kitchen; Lulu came into the library and pulled the chain of the lamp. Then she went on to other lights and other duties. Peter lay on the rug and dreamed. The camels loomed large through his half-shut eyes. Three kings were riding them, in turbans and long robes. Then someone said in a hearty way, "Asleep, Peter?"

Peter sat up. "Hello, Daddy. No, I wasn't. I was waiting for you."

"Good boy." Big Peter sat down, and young Peter leaned against his knee.

Big Peter's eyes fell on the three camels on the honey-colored rug. "It's a good thing," he said, "that you started them so soon. They have far to travel."

"Yes, they have," said Peter. His hands stole into his father's. To his mother the three toy camels would have been just three toy camels. To Daddy they were gold and frankincense and myrrh. They sat and talked together until

Mother came in. She was all dressed—beautifully—in a gown that looked like a flame.

"Oh, Daddy," she said with a sort of shining reproach. "Are you here? I thought every minute you'd be coming up. It's so late, and I had an early dinner because of the play."

"Are we going out?" Daddy got up and kissed her.

"I told you this morning—the Russians."

"I remember. Is dinner ready?"

"In fifteen minutes. I was a bit late myself. I have to fit everything in. These are busy days."

It seemed to Peter, weighing it, that his father's days were busy. He looked after people's eyes—a specialist. But he never talked about being in a hurry. "Want to come with me?" he asked Peter, and Peter followed him to the upper rooms of their spacious apartment, and watched the swift fifteen minutes of sartorial transformation, which began in a quick shower and ended with a dress coat.

While the shower was in progress, Peter gazed out the window. "It's snowing," he said when his father came back, "and the snow is funny where light shines on it."

His father, a fascinating figure in his fat blue bathrobe, and with hair wet and rumpled, took time to look. "It makes me think of an old melodrama I saw when

I was a boy, Peter. There was paper snow, and it came down on the heroine in just one spot—a handful or two—and the rest of the stage was clear—"

Peter adored his father's reminiscences. He wanted to ask more questions about the heroine out in the snow. But his father warned him. "I am in no end of a rush. Save it up, old chap, and we'll talk about it after dinner. It was a corking old play, 'Two Orphans.' "

Peter went downstairs hugging within his heart the thought of that paper storm . . . two orphans—and why was one of them out in the cold . . . ?

After dinner: "Tell me about it, Daddy."

And Mother asked, "About what?"

"Oh," said Little Peter, "something he saw at a play."

"Darling, he hasn't time. It is late as it is. And the car is waiting."

Big Peter laid his hand on his son's shoulder. "Lucia," he said, "must we go?"

"Of course. We're ready." Then the car was announced, and they went away, and Peter sat by the fire and waited for Lulu, and wished that his father were there to tell him about the orphan in the paper snow.

Big Peter's office has a succession of rooms like the sections of a telescope. You began with the great reception halls, and ended with Big Peter's tiny private office. Only special patients came into that very end room. Big Peter always opened his morning mail there, and read as much of it as he could before people came to him about their eyes. And it was the morning after he had been to see the Russians in a strange and moving play that Big Peter had a letter from his only brother, Robert. It would be, Robert said, utterly impossible for him and Jean and the boys to come down for Christmas. It was a great disappointment to them all. But that was one of the things that happened now and then to a country practitioner. One of his patients would need him on the twenty-fourth, and he and Jean had talked it over and had wondered if Big Peter and Little Peter and Lucia couldn't come up to the farm for a glorious old-fashioned Christmas Day dinner, "such as you and I had when we were boys together."

Big Peter drew a long breath. He laid the letter down and looked off into space. Then, presently, his nurse came in to announce his first patient. And Big Peter slipped into his white linen things, and scrubbed up his hands, and began his day's work. For eight hours he automatically questioned and examined and advised and gave prescriptions. And every day was just like the day before and the day after, except that on Thursday, Big Peter performed operations at the hospital. And it was not until nearly six o'clock, when he leaned back in his limousine on his way home, that Big Peter had time to think of his brother Bob's letter. It was snowing again—a new fall on the already whitened streets. There was no wind and the sounds of the city were stilled. The other cars that passed them were like shadow-shapes in the gloom. Big Peter wished that he had Little Peter beside him, wide-eyed, while they talked together of the things that had happened in Big Peter's boyhood.

Big Peter was a successful man. He and his brother, Bob, had studied medicine together, and when their father had died and the money was divided, Bob had decided to go back to the hills and take up his father's practice. Big Peter, then, had thought him foolish. The city promised so much. And it had kept its promise. Big Peter was famous. And he was not tied to things as Bob was tied. Even now, as he rode safe and warm in his great closed car, Bob might be floundering through great drifts up there in the hills.

Yet, up there in the hills, life was simpler; perhaps, after all, Bob had the best of it. Big Peter wondered what had happened to his own life—and Lucia's. Lucia was lovely. One couldn't pick a flaw in her. Yet she seemed separated from him by some intangible barrier. And she was separated, too, from Little Peter. It was noticeable how the boy shut her out from his confidence, how he left all the close and intimate things to say to his father when they were alone. And a boy shouldn't . . . A mother was a mother. Big Peter remembered his own . . . a serene person who would sit with folded hands and attentive gaze while he poured out his heart to her.

Little Peter had never been to the farm in winter. With his father and mother he had spent two weeks there one summer. Lucia had not liked it. She was city bred. She had always lived in a perfectly ordered home. Big Peter adored her, but he admitted reluctantly that at times her perfections clicked like a busy machine. That night he and Lucia dined out. Little Peter saw them off. "Don't you like her in that dress, Daddy?"

"Yes, it is your loveliest gown, Lucia."

She laughed a little. "You two . . . you are as alike as peas! I wonder why this gown takes your eye?"

"I know why it takes my eye," said Little Peter gravely. "It is like a buttercup."

"It is like a whole field of buttercups," said Big Peter.

And Lucia just laughed again and said, "Gracious, a field of buttercups sounds as big as—hoop skirts!"

It was late when Lucia and Big Peter came home from their dinner party, and it was while they sat in the library, where the fire had burned down to ashes and an opal heart, that Big Peter said, "I had a letter today from Bob."

"When are they coming?"

"They are not coming, Lucia. Bob has a case that will hold him over to the twenty-fifth. They want us to come up for the weekend and eat Christmas dinner with them."

Lucia, in the field-of-buttercups gown, leaned back against the dark leather of her chair and said, "Well, of course we can't."

"Why not?"

"You can't get away, can you?"

"Yes. McGreger will look after my patients."

She considered that for a moment. "But all our plans are made. We have so many engagements. It will be impossible to break them."

"I should like to make it possible."

She enumerated patiently. "We have accepted an invitation for the Stacys' dinner, and the Lorings', and Muriel Abbott is giving a dance, and . . ."

He lifted his hand. "Let's cut away from all of them . . . Little Peter would love it."

"But I have everything planned for Peter too. A surprise. I have asked a lot of children to come and sing carols—instead of a tree. And Peter will give them presents from a huge Christmas pie."

"Lucia, he won't like that. His tree is everything—"

She argued it and he listened, his eyes fixed frowningly on the fire. Usually he let her have her own way. He had, like Little Peter, learned the futility of argument. Lucia could everlastingly prove her point. And she was always so disturbed when he lost his temper. He did not mean to lose it now. He felt that Peter ought to have a tree. He himself wanted it. It seemed to bring to him a breath of his own pine woods. He was always sorry when New Year's Day came and the tree had to be taken down. He and Little Peter made a ceremony each year of burning it in the fireplace. "You see, it goes back up the chimney," he had told his small son, "and the wind carries it away to the forest."

"And its spirit talks to the other trees?"

"Perhaps. And tells them what it did here."

Peter and his father often talked of spirits. Big Peter

did not believe that death was the end of things. "All that is fine and good and brave in us lives forever, Peter." He wanted Little Peter to think of death without fear, and of all that came after it.

And now Lucia was saying, "Jean and Bob are great dears and the boys are darlings. But their house is terribly haphazard."

He brought himself back to her. "Oh, well, of course. If you feel that way about it, we won't think of it." He stood up. "Let's go to bed. I'm dead tired and tomorrow is my day at the hospital."

She, too, stood up. "Perhaps Little Peter can go to the farm in the spring," she said in her bright voice, "when we haven't so much going on here."

"I wasn't thinking entirely of Peter. I was thinking of . . . myself."

"Would you really like it?"

"Like it? Yes. Good Lord, yes. Why, it was home to me when I was a little chap . . ." He found it hard to go on.

Her fingertips caressed the lapel of his coat; the field-of-buttercups gown was like sunshine against the black.

"We'll go, of course. I'm not so selfish."

He was eager. "Lucia, you'll adore it. You've never seen anything like its charm in winter."

They went upstairs together, his arm around her. And he was half apologetic. "It is too bad that you'll have to spoil your plans."

Yet the last apologetic impulse died when, before going to bed, he went in and looked at Little Peter. The child was as warm and rosy as his own blue pajamas. He had crisp bronze curls, and the firm set of his chin was like Big Peter's. As the father drew up the covers, there was a rustle under his hand. Little Peter had written a note on his very own paper, with a fat gold "P" at the top. Big Peter read it under the lamp.

**Dear Santa,**

*Please bring me a tree. Mother says I am not to have one. So will you just drop it down the chimb-ley—there isn't any fire before 7 in the morning.*

*Yours truly,*
**Peter Blake**

Well, Peter should have his tree. They would have a wonderful holiday. Big Peter went back to his wife. She had taken off the yellow gown and was wrapped in something thick and warm and fur-trimmed.

"You look like a white pussycat," he told her.

"Do you like me, Peter?"

"I love you."

It is one thing, however, to agree to a plan of which you don't exactly approve, and it is another thing to adjust yourself to it. Little Peter's raptures when he heard of their trip to the farm puzzled his mother.

"But how do you know you are going to like it, Peter?"

"Well, Daddy has told me about it."

"You may not like it as well as Daddy did."

"Yes, I shall, Mother. Father says I can sit in the kitchen and watch Aunt Jean make doughnuts and sprinkle them with sugar when they come out of the fat. He used to do it when he was a little boy."

"But, darling, you know you are not allowed to eat doughnuts."

"Well, Daddy said I might, up there. He said if I walked a lot and cut down Christmas trees that even doughnuts wouldn't hurt my tummy."

"Did he say that you could cut down Christmas trees?"

"He said I could help." Little Peter's cheeks were scarlet with the excitement of it all. Lucia sighed. She wished that Big Peter wouldn't upset her diet arrangements for her son.

She was having a great many notes to write, and explanations to make over the telephone. It seemed best to say that Big Peter needed a rest. She told that to the Lorings and the Stacys and to Muriel Abbott. They were all very sorry for her. Maude Maddox agreed to take the two old ladies from the home off her hands. The children who were to have sung the carols were given a little party on the day before Peter went away. The whole thing was perfectly managed, and all the mothers praised Lucia. After everybody had gone home, Little Peter was very polite about it. "They had a nice time, didn't they, Mother."

She was moved, unexpectedly, to ask, "Did you?"

Truth got the better of politeness, "Not so very."

"But why not, Peter?"

"Oh, it was like all other parties, Mother."

She stared at him, a little frown fretting her forehead. His words were an echo of his father's as they had driven home one night from a country club party. "They are all alike, Lucia. And nothing seems real."

She had wondered then what he meant by "real." As for herself, she had been chair of the committee, and things had really been very well done. And everybody had been pleased except Big Peter, who called it "artificial" and "cut-and-dried."

"It would have been hopeless without the cocktails."

"But you didn't drink any, Peter."

"I never do. And neither do you. Yet you seem to get a lot out of it."

Lucia was quite sure that Big Peter ought to get a lot out of it too. But he didn't, and now here was Little Peter!

She packed their bags with warm things, thick sweaters, and underwear. "I can't have my two Peters taking cold," she told them, "and those old country houses are apt to be freezing." She need not have worried, however. Uncle Bob's house was warm enough. Little Peter felt that it was warm not only to your outside feelings, but to those inside you. You went straight into the lamp-lighted front room, and there were three cats on the hearth. The fire was back of them and the cats looked black. But when you came up to them, they were three colors—one was gray and one was black and one was a bright and beautiful yellow.

Little Peter took the yellow cat on his lap. "I haven't had one since I was here that summer," he said to his aunt Jean.

"There are more of them out in the barn."

Little Peter felt that he could sit there forever with

that warm, fat pussycat in his arms. But his mother was saying, "May I put Peter to bed? It is so late for him."

"Doesn't he want something to eat?"

"We had dinner in the dining car, Jean."

"But I *do* want something to eat, Mother."

"Peter!" Then gravely, "Well, a glass of milk," and Peter put down his cat and went with his aunt to get it.

They had to walk down three steps to the dairy; and there, around the wall of the broad shelves, were pans of milk and all the room was sweet with the smell of it. And the floor was painted yellow, just the color of the cat, and the cream was yellow. And there was a dipper and a glass. While he drank his milk, Little Peter talked to his aunt Jean. He didn't feel shy and he liked the way she listened. She seemed to put her mind to it, as his father did.

"We haven't any cats," Little Peter told her, "or any animals."

"Our pets are just a part of the family. There's Old Caesar. He goes everywhere with your uncle, and the people know the dog as well as the doctor . . . and there's young Brutus, who watches the house. And there's Tessie, the old tortoiseshell pussy. She keeps her kittens at the barn. And it is always a great ceremony when she brings them up to be fed. We all go out to see them. And she is so proud!"

"At home," said Peter, "I have my Noah's Ark, but of course the animals are not alive."

"Still," said Aunt Jean understandingly, "they are a great help. You can play they are real."

"That's what I do." Peter found himself telling about the camels on the honey-colored rug. "Three kings . . ."

Aunt Jean nodded. "Do you know," she said, and Peter thought she was a very beautiful lady in her blue linen dress, with her shining hair and attentive blue eyes. "Do you know, I have often wondered what the animals thought when they first saw the Child."

"They fell on their knees," Peter elucidated.

She smiled. "That's just a legend, isn't it?"

"Well, Daddy says some people believe that they kneel down on Christmas night."

"Do you believe?"

Little Peter had finished his milk. He handed the glass to Aunt Jean. "Thank you," he said. Then, carefully, "They might kneel, you know."

He tucked his hand in hers as they went up the three steps together. He felt that he had had a very wonderful visit with Aunt Jean in the milk room. And they were very well acquainted. It was as if he had lived with her all his life.

The two days before Christmas were tremendously interesting to Little Peter.

It was joyful adventure to get up early and help feed and water the stock, and watch the milking with Uncle Bob's three boys. Their names were Oliver and George and Theodore. Little Peter's mother thought that the boys' names should have been different. "Why didn't you carry on the family line?"

Aunt Jean smiled. "We decided to start a new one. We don't intend that our boys shall ever blame their ancestors for anything. We want them to think about their descendants."

"How queer," said Little Peter's mother.

"Well, it does sound queer," said Aunt Jean, "but they have three big names to live up to and they seem to like it."

The boys drove a fat little horse into town every morning to school. But the fat little horse was now having his holiday with the rest of them. He went up in the woods to help bring back the tree. Little Peter rode on his back part of the way. His father walked beside them, and the snow sparkled, and all the lovely young pines seemed like human beings as they stood tall and straight in the sunshine. Little Peter winced when the ax cut into the trunk of one of the trees. His father saw it and said, "Isn't it better to die as a Christmas tree than to be mown down in a storm and rot on the ground?"

And later Peter's father said to Uncle Bob, "That's the trouble in town . . . he has no contact with reality. Out here, among all the living things, life and death take on their proper proportions. I don't want him to shrink neurotically from the thought of pain and poverty and dissolution. I want him to accept them as a part of things—unafraid."

Getting ready for Christmas in his aunt Jean's kitchen, Little Peter found a great event. One didn't just telephone to the butcher and baker and confectioner and have things quite magically brought to one's back door. Aunt Jean and her Swedish maid, Olga, baked the bread, and baked the cakes, and baked the pies; and the turnips and potatoes and onions were brought up from bins in the cellar, and the pickled peaches and jellies and mincemeat came down from the shelves of Aunt Jean's pantry. And the turkey! But that was the tragedy! The turkey came right out of a beautiful flock, all shining bronze, that Peter had seen in the sunshine! And Peter had to be consoled. Peter sat in the kitchen and watched Aunt Jean make the mince pies. He thought the coal range much nicer than the gas range at home. The fire glowed in it and it gave out warmth and its great ovens baked loaves and loaves and loaves of the loveliest bread.

He liked the way, too, that Aunt Jean and Olga served the meals. They had two courses, and there were great dishes of potatoes and great bowls of gravy and great platters of meat . . . and everything was on the table at once except the dessert. And Uncle Bob said grace, and the grace that he said was this: "O Lord, make us strong men and good men, and strong women and good women. For Christ's sake, Amen." And he said this three times a day.

It seemed to Little Peter that one just had to be strong and good when one heard things like that three times a day in Uncle Bob's hearty voice.

He talked it over with his father. "Why don't you say it at our house?"

"Your mother likes the one I say better."

Little Peter was polite. "Oh, well, of course. Yours is nice . . . but Uncle Bob's sticks in your mind."

There was one thing that Big Peter had promised. They were to go out to the barn at midnight on Christmas Eve. There was a chance, Little Peter had said, that the animals might kneel.

"You mustn't be disappointed if they don't," his father told him.

"Well, I won't be. It's just a legend," said Little Peter, quoting Aunt Jean, "but then, you know, Daddy . . . they *might.*"

Peter found that while Aunt Jean was a very busy woman, she was not busy in the way that his mother was. She always seemed to find time for her boys and for Uncle Bob. When they came in, she would drift to the fire and the chintz chair, and sit there while they told her the news, or asked her opinion, or relieved their minds of some burden of thought. And at night she sat by the fire and knitted while the boys read aloud, or Uncle Bob told them all of his day's work.

"She reminds me," said Big Peter, "of my mother."

"She reminds me," said Lucia with unexpected spite, "of a tranquil cow."

"There are worse things," said Big Peter, "than a tranquil cow," and tried to laugh it off.

But he couldn't quite, and Lucia couldn't laugh either. And for a long time they were silent, and at last she said, "I don't know what is the matter with me to say a thing like that."

But the thing that was the matter with Lucia was jealousy, although she didn't know it—jealousy, green-eyed, jaundiced.

And she was jealous of Aunt Jean! At first she hadn't been. She had felt superior. And self-satisfied. She knew that she was prettier than Aunt Jean. And better dressed. And her house was well ordered. And Little Peter's manners were perfect. And for the first few hours after she arrived, she had quite wanted to patronize Aunt Jean, and to tell her how to do things—how to run her house like clockwork, and how to teach old Olga to wait on the table, how to manage Uncle Bob so he wouldn't say that odd grace. And she had felt that all that food on the table at once was a mistake. People didn't eat that way anymore. Not so heartily and heavily. There could be less informality, more exquisiteness; Jean was carrying simplicity to excess.

But after two days of it, Lucia began to feel that perhaps Jean was wiser than she had seemed. For Aunt Jean was like a sun around which her small world revolved. Her boys adored her. Her husband adored her. Bob never came in from his rounds without shouting, "Where's Jeannie?" and greeting her as if they had been parted for ages. His eyes shone for her. He was her comrade, her lover.

As for the boys. To see them at her feet while she knitted—young Ted's rough head against her knee, the light in Oliver's glance as it met hers, the affectionate assurance with which young George demanded her opinion and got it—was to see a queen in her own domain. And Lucia was not a queen. She was, rather, dictator. But Peter and Little Peter did what she wanted them to do. But they did it listlessly. At times they seemed to draw away from her. More and more they talked together, shut her out. As for her competency, didn't it consist merely in making up lists and ordering other people to do things? She had expert maids and an expert modiste. She couldn't make a dress. She couldn't cook a meal. She couldn't sweep a room or keep a set of books. And Jean could do all of these things.

But that didn't so much matter. The thing that mattered was that Jean was the sun who lighted her own small world. Lucia envied her that. Of course being a sun in a city apartment presented some difficulties. She wondered what Jean would do if she lived in town. She made up her mind to ask her.

It was the night before Christmas. The tree was set up in the living room, and there was the thick, spicy smell of it, which Little Peter loved. And late in the afternoon Little Peter and his cousins had popped corn while the snow came down outside and they had strung it into chains, and while they had strung the chains they had talked about names.

His cousins' names had always seemed to Little Peter to be quite curious and satisfying. He felt that it must be very interesting to know that you were Oliver *Cromwell* Blake and George *Washington* Blake, and Theodore *Roosevelt* Blake.

"I am just Peter," he said, "like my father and grandfather."

"No," said Aunt Jean, who was knitting in her chintz chair. "You are Peter not only like your father and grandfather, but you are like Peter of the Rock."

"Who was he, Aunt Jean?"

"Read about him, Oliver."

So Oliver read from a big, shabby book, "Thou art

Peter, and upon this rock I will build my church; and the gates of hell shall not prevail against it."

And Peter, listening, felt tremendously thrilled. Not that he quite understood. But he understood enough to know that Peter of the Rock must be rather splendid to be named for—more splendid even than Cromwell or Washington or Roosevelt.

Then Lucia, who was sitting back in the shadows, said, "Jean, I don't see how you do it."

"Do what?"

"Make yourself one of them."

"It is easy enough," said Aunt Jean, "if you take time for it."

Lucia wanted to say *How can one take time in a city apartment?* But just then Uncle Bob came in, and Big Peter, and Uncle Bob had to have his supper at once. He was called out on a case, and Big Peter was going with him. "It is an operation and he can help me a lot. Up here in the hills it is hard to get anyone."

They had a hearty supper, and after supper, while Little Peter was feeding the cats in the pump room, his father appeared in the doorway. He had on a fur coat and a fur cap, and he looked like a bear. "I'm sorry, old chap," he said, "I may not get back in time to go to the barn."

Little Peter straightened up. "Well, of course, if you can't, you can't."

"That's the way to take it. I'll get here if possible."

Little Peter went out and watched his father and Uncle Bob drive away. They were in a high-powered car that had been Big Peter's Christmas present to his brother. "One fee paid for it," he had said when Bob had protested. "I kept a millionaire from going blind."

"Great stuff," said Bob.

"But you don't envy me?"

Bob had shaken his head. "Each man to his own job; I am used to this."

The old dog, Caesar, was curled up under a rug on the backseat as they drove away. He was getting very old and it was a cold night, but he always howled when he was left behind.

After the men were gone, Aunt Jean and Little Peter's mother turned the young people out of the living room and trimmed the tree. And Little Peter and his cousins went into the kitchen to make candy. It was really a most entrancing occupation. On the glowing range was a great saucepan full of molasses and sugar and butter. It boiled and bubbled and the whole place was soon filled with the satisfying fragrance. And there were big white platters with nut meats on them. And you poured some of the taffy over the nut meats, and some of it you pulled. And it was while Little Peter and his cousins pulled the taffy that Lucia, tying a pink angel to the top of the tree, looked down at Jean and said, "If you lived in an apartment, what would you do?"

Jean looked up at her and laughed. "I'd move."

"I don't mean that. What would you do about living? I've been watching you and the boys and Bob. You are the center of their world. And I am not the center of mine."

"Well, it is this way," said Jean. "Bob and the boys are so interesting to me that nothing else counts."

"Do you mean that you like it so much?"

"Yes, they are full of the wine of life. When I am with them, I seem to drink of it."

Lucia argued, "If you lived in the city, you'd have to do as the Romans do."

"There would be a difference, of course," Jean admitted, "but the main thing is to get the right attitude of mind. Bob and the boys are my most gorgeous adventure. And they know it. So they open the gates of their dreams, and off we go together!"

Lucia looked down from the stepladder. "Little Peter has shut the gate of his dreams and locked me out."

"The key is in your own heart, Lucia," Jean said. "When your two Peters become the most important thing in the world to you, you'll become the most important thing to them."

Then, after a moment, she added, "I always think of my boys as potential leaders of men. I want them to be that. I think they will be."

Lucia came down from the stepladder. "It is Peter's bedtime." She laid her hand on Jean's shoulder. "Do you know that you are a most inspiring person?"

Jean reached up and patted the slender hand. "I know that you are a most beautiful one."

"Oh, *beauty*," said Lucia, "half of it is my clothes!"

Little Peter went to bed but not to sleep. It was a tall bed with four posts, and a blue and white quilt with a fringe. It had stopped snowing, and the open window made a square of clear blue light. The door that led to his mother's room was a golden space in which he could see her moving back and forth. She had on her warm, thick pussycat robe. Peter liked the pussycat robe and so did his father. It had white fur at the neck and wrists. He heard his mother open her own window, then she came to the door. "Sleep, Peter?"

"No."

She bent above the bed. "I kissed you once, didn't I?

Well, I'll kiss you twice, and three times, and then you must close your eyes."

She knelt with her arms around him. "And when you wake, it will be Christmas morning."

Peter knew that he would wake long before that. He was going out to the barn to see what the animals would do at midnight. If Daddy came, so much the better. But he wasn't going to lose this chance to see whether the cows and the horses and the old sheep who churned the butter would kneel.

For one moment he was tempted to ask his mother to go with him. But he knew what she would say: *How silly— to think that the animals* would. And that would spoil it.

He slept before he knew it and waked with a start. He wondered if it was midnight, and even while he wondered he heard the grandfather's clock in the lower hall strike with a jangle of chimes—eleven. He lay, then, waiting until another brief jangle marked the quarter after. He climbed out of bed, gathered up his clothes, and in his bare feet descended the stairs and made his way to the living room.

It was all shadowy with the glow of the dim lamp and of the deep-hearted coals. The cats were curled up in a warm heap on the rug. The room was deliciously cozy after the keen air upstairs. He sat on the rug among the little cats and donned his stockings hastily, his shoes and under-clothes, his knickers and jacket. Then he pulled over all his thick sweater, and covered his ears with his knitted cap. He found a pencil and wrote a note which he propped up against the lamp:

**Dear Daddy,**

*I've gone to the barn. I thought I'd better not wait. I hope you will come.*

**Peter**

He felt very daring as he opened the door and went out into the night. The sky was powdered with stars; it seemed very high and different from the sky in the city, which was always blurred by the electric lights.

Young Brutus, the watchdog, came out of his kennel and trotted over the frozen snow ahead of Peter. He made no sound, and in the clear dark he looked long and lean, like a wolf. But Little Peter was not afraid of him. He was, indeed, glad of his company.

The barn was lighted by a single lantern. Back among the shadows were the cows, comfortable on beds of straw. The old butter-sheep and a blind mare had open stalls to themselves. Beyond them were the strong workhorses and the lighter span which the doctor drove now and then. Tessie, the barn cat, came down to investigate the invasion. Peter sat on a feed box and took her in his lap and waited. It seemed wonderful to sit there in the company of all these living creatures—and to know that there were pigeons up among the rafters, and Tessie's kittens in the loft. There was a round barn clock, and it showed a quarter of twelve. Peter felt a tingling sense of excitement. Something must, he felt, in a moment, happen.

And now young Brutus was on his feet—stiff and suspicious—his eyes on the side door by which Peter had entered. The door opened. And Peter saw a woman coming in. She wore a long blue cloak and carried a lantern. There was a scarf over her head which hid her face.

Peter knew at once why she had come. She was tired. . . and there was no room for her at the inn. . . .

He rose to his feet and stood for a moment, uncertain, then sent a breathless little cry across the intervening space. *"Mary!"*

Lucia had waked to find Peter gone. She had slipped into the pussycat robe and had sought him downstairs. She had found the note propped up against the lamp. She had dressed hurriedly. The blue cloak and scarf she had borrowed from the hall rack. They belonged to Jean, and fell about her own slender figure in voluminous folds.

She had lighted a lantern and made her way to the barn. And now she was saying, her own breath quick, "It is Mother, darling," and Peter with dreams still in his eyes was stammering, "Why, I didn't know you!"

"Why did you come, Peter?"

"Well, I thought they might kneel—the animals, you know."

"Oh, at midnight?"

"Yes."

She glanced up at the clock. "Five minutes."

He was anxious. "May I stay?"

"Yes. Shall we sit here?" The feed box was wide enough for both of them. She put her arm around Peter and he leaned against her. The blue cloak enfolded them; the lantern held them close in its circle of light.

In the moments that followed, the silence seemed to Lucia to flow up and around them in warm and shining waves. She was aware of all the living things so near them in the dark. Shut away from the clamor of her own quick and changing world, she seemed to share something with these dumb and tranquil beasts.

Tranquility! Was it that she had missed? Would Little Peter and Big Peter draw close if she shut them into a world of her own where peace reigned? And could they shut her out if she shut them in?

Little Peter's breathless cry had moved her strangely. He had linked her by his vivid imagination to that other Mother, had bridged two thousand years and brought her close to that serene and gracious presence.

"Mother, it's twelve!" Little Peter's hand clutched her arm. "It's twelve!"

The old clock ticked a round of sixty seconds, another round. Little Peter was on his feet, his eager eyes sweeping the shadows, where dark outlines loomed, unmoving and unchanged.

At last he drew a long, quivering breath. "Oh, they didn't do it, Mother."

She felt she must not fail him. "Darling," she said, "perhaps they knelt—in their hearts."

Far back in his eyes there danced a light, the light

that had shone hitherto only for Big Peter. His warm hand went into hers. He gave a contented little laugh. "Oh, well, it was wonderful to come, wasn't it?"

It was more wonderful than he knew.

And now across the small-paned windows swept the streaming gold of headlights, and there was the purr of the engine. Silence. Then the great door slid back and Big Peter peered in. "Who's here?"

Little Peter gave a great shout and fell upon him. "It's Mother, Daddy, and me."

"Lucia?"

She came forward. "Yes. Where's Bob?"

"He stayed all night." Big Peter's voice trailed away. He stood staring. Lucia in that blue cloak among the golden shadows. Why, the thing was like an old painting! "Do you know," he asked abruptly, "that you make me think of the Madonna?"

"Little Peter saw it too," she said. She laid her hand on his arm, looking up at him. "When I came in he called me . . . Mary."

He was at once aware that she was deeply moved. His own heartbeats quickened. His arms went around her. "All mothers are Marys, my darling." She leaned her head against him, loving his tenderness. She put her arm around Little Peter and he leaned against her. The blue cloak enfolded them. With the child they stood in the circle of light made by the lantern.

And it was Christmas morning!

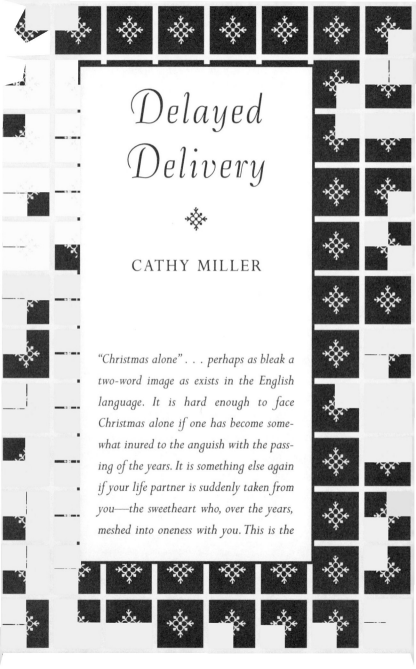

# Delayed Delivery

❄

## CATHY MILLER

"Christmas alone" . . . perhaps as bleak a two-word image as exists in the English language. It is hard enough to face Christmas alone if one has become some-what inured to the anguish with the passing of the years. It is something else again if your life partner is suddenly taken from you—the sweetheart who, over the years, meshed into oneness with you. This is the

*sorrow America's greatest poetess, Emily Dickinson, was thinking*
*of when she wrote*

> *The sweeping up the Heart*
> *And putting Love away*
> *We shall not want to use again*
> *Until Eternity.*

*A Canadian teacher and freelance writer responded to a* *1992 Christmas story contest in her area newspaper,* Northern Life. *Her story won first prize. Mrs. Maimu Veedler, of Lively, Ontario, was given a copy of* Christmas in My Heart, *and responding to my call for extra special stories, sent me a copy of this prize-winning story. I called the genial editor, Ms. Carol Mulligan, who in turn contacted Mrs. Miller of Sudbury, Ontario. Mrs. Miller called me—and permission was granted for the inclusion of this moving story of a delayed gift which arrived at just the right time.*

*Since Dr. James Dobson used this as the Focus on the Family Christmas story of the year in 1994, it has become a treasured part of the season with tens of thousands all around the world.*

There had never been a winter like this. Stella watched from the haven of her armchair as gusts of snow whipped themselves into a frenzy. She feared to stand close to the window, unreasonably afraid that somehow the blizzard might be able to reach her there, sucking her, breathless, out into the chaos. The houses across the street were all but obliterated by the fury of windborne flakes. Absently, the elderly woman straightened the slipcovers on the arms of her chair, her eyes glued to the spectacle beyond the glass.

Dragging her gaze away from the window, she forced herself up out of her chair and waited a moment for balance to reassert itself. Straightening her back against the pain that threatened to keep her stooped, she set out determinedly for the kitchen.

In the doorway to the next room she paused, her mind blank, wondering what purpose had propelled her there. From the vent above the stove the scream of the wind threatened to funnel the afternoon storm directly down into the tiny house. Stella focused brown eyes on the stovetop clock. The three-fifteen time reminded her that she had headed in there to take something out of the freezer for her supper. Another lonely meal that she didn't feel like preparing, much less eating.

Suddenly she grabbed the handle of the refrigerator and leaned her forehead against the cold white surface of the door as a wave of self-pity threatened to drown her. It was too much to bear, losing her beloved Dave this summer! How as she to endure the pain, the daily nothingness? She felt the familiar ache in her throat and squeezed her eyes tightly shut to hold the tears at bay.

Stella drew herself upright and shook her head in silent chastisement. She reiterated her litany of thanks. She had her health, her tiny home, an income that would suffice for the remainder of her days. She had her books, her television programs, her needlework. There were the pleasures of her garden in the spring and summer, walks through the wilderness park at the end of her street, and the winter birds that brightened the feeders outside her kitchen picture window. *Not today though,* she thought ruefully as the blizzard hurled itself against the eastern wall of the kitchen.

"Ah, Dave, I miss you so! I never minded storms when you were here." The sound of her own voice echoed hollowly in the room. She turned on the radio that stood on the counter next to a neatly descending row of wooden canisters. A sudden joyful chorus of Christmas music filled the room, but it served only to deepen her loneliness.

Stella had been prepared for her husband's death. Since the doctor's pronouncement of terminal lung cancer, they had both faced the inevitable, striving to make the most of their remaining time together. Dave's financial affairs had always been in order. There were no new burdens in her widowed state. It was just the awful aloneness . . . the lack of purpose to her days.

They had been a childless couple. It had been their choice. Their lives had been full and rich. They had been content with busy careers, and with each other.

They had had many friends. *Had.* That was the operative word these days. It was bad enough losing the one person you loved with all your heart. But over the last few years she and Dave repeatedly had to cope with the deaths of their friends and relations. They were all of an age——the age when human bodies began giving up—dying. Face it, they were old!

And now, on this first Christmas without Dave, Stella would be on her own. Mabel and Jim had invited her to spend the holiday with them in Florida, but somehow that had seemed worse than staying at home alone. Not only would she miss her husband, she would miss the snow and the winter and the familiarity of her home.

With shaky fingers she lowered the volume of the radio so that the music became a muted background. She glanced toward the fridge briefly, then decided that a hot bowl of soup would be more comforting fare this evening.

To her surprise, she saw that the mail had come. She hadn't even heard the creak of the levered mail slot in the front door. Poor mailman, out in this weather! "Neither hail, nor sleet . . ." With the inevitable wince of pain she bent to retrieve the damp white envelopes from the floor. Moving into the living room, she sat on the piano bench to open them. They were mostly Christmas cards, and her sad eyes smiled at the familiarity of the traditional scenes and at the loving messages inside. Carefully, her arthritic fingers arranged them among the others clustered on the piano top. In her entire house they were the only seasonal decoration. The holiday was less than a week away, but she just did not have the heart to put up a silly tree, or even set up the stable that Dave had built with his own hands.

Suddenly engulfed by the loneliness of it all, Stella buried her lined face in her hands, lowering her elbows to the piano keys in a harsh, abrasive discord, and let the tears come. How would she possibly get through Christmas and the winter beyond it? She longed to climb into bed and bury herself in a cocoon of blankets, not emerging until her friends and spring returned.

The ring of the doorbell echoed the high-pitched, discordant piano notes and was so unexpected that Stella had to stifle a small scream of surprise. Now, who could possibly be calling on her on a day like today? Wiping her eyes, she noticed for the first time how dark the room had become. The doorbell sounded a second time.

Using the piano for leverage, she raised herself upright and headed for the front hall, switching on the living room light as she passed. She opened the wooden door and stared through the screened window of the storm door in consternation. On her front porch, buffeted by waves of wind and snow, stood a strange young man whose hatless head was barely visible above the large carton in his arms. She peered beyond him to the driveway, but there was nothing about the small car to give clue to his identity. Returning her gaze to him, she saw that his hands were bare and his eyebrows had lifted in an expression of hopeful appeal that was fast disappearing behind the frost forming on the glass. Summoning courage, the elderly lady opened the door slightly and he stepped sideways to speak into the space.

"Mrs. Thornhope?"

She nodded affirmation, her extended arm beginning to tremble with cold and the strain of holding the door against the wind. He continued predictably, "I have a package for you."

Curiosity drove warning thoughts from her mind. She pushed the door far enough to enable the stranger to shoulder it and stepped back into the foyer to make room for him. He entered, bringing with him the frozen breath of the storm. Smiling, he placed his burden carefully on the floor and stood to retrieve an envelope that protruded from his pocket. As he handed it to her, a sound came from the box. Stella actually jumped. The man laughed in apology and bent to straighten up the cardboard flaps, holding them open in an invitation for her to peek inside. She advanced cautiously, then turned her gaze downward.

It was a dog! To be more exact, a golden Labrador retriever puppy. As the gentleman lifted its squirming body up into his arms, he explained, "This is for you, ma'am. He's six weeks old and completely housebroken." The young pup wiggled in happiness at being released from captivity and thrust ecstatic, wet kisses in the direction of his benefactor's chin. "We were supposed to deliver him on Christmas Eve," he continued with some difficulty as he strove to rescue his chin from the wet little tongue, "but the staff at the kennels start their holidays tomorrow. Hope you don't mind an early present."

Shock had stolen her ability to think clearly. Unable to form coherent sentences, she stammered, "But . . . I don't . . . I mean . . . who . . . ?" The young fellow set the animal down on the doormat between them and then reached out a finger to tap the envelope she was still holding.

"There's a letter in there that explains everything, pretty much. The dog was bought last July while her mother was still pregnant. It was meant to be a Christmas gift. If you'll just wait a minute, there are some things in the car I'll get for you."

Before she could protest, he was gone, returning a moment later with a huge box of dog food, a leash, and a book titled *Caring for Your Labrador Retriever.* All this time the puppy had sat quietly at her feet, panting happily as his brown eyes watched her.

Unbelievably, the stranger was turning to go. Desperation forced the words from her lips. "But who . . . who bought it?" Pausing in the open doorway, his words almost snatched away by the wind that tousled his hair, he replied, "Your husband, ma'am." And then he was gone.

It was all in the letter. Forgetting the puppy entirely at this sight of the familiar handwriting, Stella had walked like a somnambulist to her chair by the window. Unaware that the little dog had followed her, she forced tear-filled eyes to read her husband's words. He had written it three weeks before his death and had left it with the kennel owners to be delivered along with the puppy as his last Christmas gift to her. It was full of love and encourage-ment and admonishments to be strong. He vowed that he was waiting somewhere for the day when she would join him. And he had sent her this young animal to keep her company until then.

Remembering the little creature for the first time, she was surprised to find him quietly looking up at her, his small, panting mouth resembling a comic smile. Stella put the pages aside and reached down for the bundle of golden fur. She had thought he would be heavier, but he was only the size and weight of a sofa pillow. And so soft and warm. She cradled him in her arms and he licked her jawbone, then cuddled up into the hollow of her neck. The tears began anew at this exchange of affection, and the dog endured her crying without moving.

Finally, Stella lowered him to her lap, where he regarded her solemnly. She wiped vaguely at her wet cheeks, then somehow mustered a smile.

"Well, little guy. I guess it's you and me." His pink tongue panted in agreement. Stella's smile strengthened and her gaze shifted sideways to the window. Dusk had fallen and the storm seemed to have spent the worst of its fury. Through fluffy flakes that were now drifting down at a gentler pace, she saw the cheery Christmas lights that edged the rooflines of her neighbors' homes. The strains of "Joy to the World" wafted in from the kitchen.

Suddenly Stella felt the most amazing sensation of peace and benediction washing over her. It was like being enfolded in a loving embrace. Her heart beat painfully, but it was with joy and wonder, not grief or loneliness. She need never feel alone again. Returning her attention to the dog, she spoke to him. "You know, fella, I have a box in the basement that I think you'd like. There's a tree in it and some decorations and lights that will impress you like crazy! And I think I can find that old stable down there too. What d'ya say we go hunt it up?" The puppy barked happily in agreement, as if he understood every word.

# The Tallest Angel

❖

## AUTHOR UNKNOWN

*Some stories are like a well-loved and mauled teddy bear: They achieve an esoteric value far above their market value—this is just such a story. It has warmed my heart and scolded me ever since I first heard it many years ago. It is one of those stories that surreptitiously grows on you, preying on your subconscious, and jerking you out of your smug self-righteousness.*

*Why? Because it hits us in one of our most vulnerable spots: how we treat the unlovely among us. Let's face it: It's as hard not to care for the beautiful ones as it is to care for the unattractive and unresponsive*

*This story graphically reveals the almost awesome power a teacher has to change lives, both by default and overt act.*

*Just as we could profit with rereading I Corinthians XIII every day of our lives, so could we with this story. Were we to do so, this would be a far different and more caring world in which to live.*

"God doesn't love me!" The words echoed sharply through the thoughts of Miss Ellis as she looked around the fourth-grade schoolroom. Her gaze skipped lightly over the many bent heads and then rested on one in particular. "God doesn't love me!" The words had struck her mind so painfully that her mouth opened slightly in mute protest.

The child under Miss Ellis's troubled study lifted her head for a moment, scanned her classmates briefly, then bent to her book again.

Ever since the first day of school, Miss Ellis had been

hurt and troubled by those bitter assertions. "God doesn't love me!" The words had come from the small nine-year-old girl who stirred again restively under the continued scrutiny of Miss Ellis. Then, bending her head to her own desk, Miss Ellis prayed in her heart for the nth time: *Help her, dear God, and help me to help her. Please show Dory that you do love her too.*

Dory sat with her geography book open upon her desk, but the thoughts that raced through her mind were not concerned with the capital of Ohio. A moment before, she had felt the warm eyes of Miss Ellis upon her, and now angry sentences played tag with each other in her bowed head. Once again she heard the calm voice of Miss Ellis.

"God wants us to be happy in His love." Dory laughed bitterly to herself. How could anyone be happy with a hunched back and leg braces!

"God loves everyone," Miss Ellis had said, to which Dory had angrily replied, "But he doesn't love me—that's why He made me ugly and crippled."

"God is good."

"God is not good to me. He's mean to me! That's what—to let me grow so crooked."

Dory raised her head and looked at the children around her. Mary Ann had long, golden curls; Dory had

125

straight brown hair, pulled back tight and braided into an unlovely pigtail. Jeanetta had china-blue eyes that twinkled like evening stars; Dory had brown eyes that seemed smoky, so full of bitterness were they. Ellen Sue had a pink rosebud mouth that readily spread into a happy smile. Well, Ellen Sue could smile. She had a lovely dimpled face and ruffled, ribboned dresses. But why should Dory smile? Her mouth was straight and tight, and her body hunched and twisted. Anyone would laugh to see ruffles on *her* dresses. No pink and blue dresses for her, only straight dark gowns that hung like sacks over her small, hunched frame.

Suddenly hate and anger so filled the heart of the little girl that she felt she must get away from this roomful of straight-bodied children or choke. She signaled her desire to Miss Ellis, who nodded permission.

There was neither pity nor laughter in the eyes that followed Dory to the door, only casual indifference. The children had long since accepted Dory as she was. No one ever jeered at her awkwardness, nor did anyone fuss over her in pity. The children did not mean to be unkind, but knowing the limits of Dory's mobility, they usually ran off to their active games, leaving her a lonely little spectator.

Miss Ellis saw the children settle back to their studies as the door closed after Dory. She stared at the door, not seeing the door at all, only the small, hunchbacked girl.

*What can I do to help her to be happy?* she pondered. *What can anyone say or do to comfort and encourage such a child?*

She had talked to Dory's parents and had found them to be of little help. They seemed inclined to feel that Dory's crippled condition was a blot upon them, one they did not deserve. Miss Ellis had urged them not to try to explain Dory's condition but to accept it as God's will and try to seek His blessings through acceptance of His will. They were almost scornful to the idea that any blessing could be found in a crippled, unhappy child, but they did agree to come to church and to bring Dory as often as possible.

*Please help Dory,* prayed Miss Ellis, *help Dory and her parents too.* Then the hall bell sounded, and Miss Ellis arose to dismiss her class.

The reds, yellows, and greens of autumn faded into the white of winter. The Christmas season was unfolding in the room. Tiny Christmas trees stood shyly on the windowsills. A great green wreath covered the door. Its silver bells jingled whenever the door moved, and the delighted giggles of the children echoed in return. The blue-white shadows of a winter afternoon were creeping across the snow as Miss Ellis watched the excited children set up the manger scene on the low sand table.

*Christmas,* thought Miss Ellis, *is a time of peace and joy. Even the children feel the spirit and try to be nicer to one another.*

"Is your Christmas dress done yet, Ellen Sue?"

Without waiting for an answer, Mary Ann chattered on. "Mother got material for mine today—it's red, real red velvet. Oh, I can hardly wait, can you?"

"Mine is all done but the hem." Ellen Sue fairly trembled with excitement. "It's pink, with rosebuds made of ribbon."

Miss Ellis smiled, remembering the thrill of the Christmas dresses of her own girlhood. How carefully they were planned, and how lovingly her mother had made each one. Miss Ellis leaned back to cherish the memories a moment longer. Then a movement caught her eye. Slowly, furtively, with storm-filled eyes, Dory was backing away from the chattering children. Her heart stirred with sympathy, Miss Ellis watched the unhappy child ease herself into her chair, pull a book from her desk, and bend her head over it. *She isn't studying,* thought Miss Ellis. *She is only pretending—to cover up her misery.*

Dory stared at the book in front of her, fighting

against the tears that demanded release. What if one of the girls had asked about *her* Christmas dress? Her Christmas dress indeed! Would anyone call a brown sack of a dress a Christmas dress? Would the children laugh? No, Dory knew the girls wouldn't laugh. They would just feel sorry for her and her shapeless dress. Sometimes that was almost worse than if they would laugh. At least then she would have an excuse to pour out the angry words that crowded into her throat.

"Dory." A warm voice broke in upon her thoughts. "Dory, will you help me with these Christmas decorations? You could walk along and hold them for me while I pin them up, please."

Dory arose, thankful for the diversion and thankful to be near Miss Ellis. The silver tinsel was pleasant to hold, and Miss Ellis always made her feel so much better.

Slowly, they proceeded around the room, draping the tinsel garlands as they went. The babble of voices in the corner by the sand table took on a new note, an insistent clamoring tone that finally burst forth in a rush of small bodies in the direction of Miss Ellis.

"Please, Miss Ellis, can I be Mary in the Christmas program?"

"Miss Ellis, I'd like to be Joseph."

"I should be Mary because I can't sing in the angel choir."

Miss Ellis raised her hand for quiet. After a moment she said, "I've already chosen the ones who will play the parts of Mary, Joseph, the shepherds, and the angel choir."

"Tell us the names; tell us the names now," the children chorused.

"All right," agreed Miss Ellis as she reached for a piece of paper from her desk. "Here they are: Sue Ellen will be Mary; Daniel will be Joseph; John, Allen, and Morris will be the shepherds. All the rest of you will be choir angels—"

Miss Ellis scanned the eager, hopeful faces around her till she saw the upturned face of Dory. There was no eager hope in her small, pinched face. Dory felt from bitter experience that no one wanted a hunchback in a program. Miss Ellis could not bear the numb resignation on that small, white face. Almost without realizing what she was saying, she finished the sentence. "All will be choir angels except Dory." There was a moment of hushed surprise. "Dory will be the special angel who talks to the shepherds."

All the children gasped and turned to look at Dory.

Dory, a special angel? They had never thought of that. As realization penetrated Dory's amazement, a slow smile relaxed the pinched features, a little candle flame of happiness shone in the brown eyes.

*Her eyes are lovely when she's happy,* marveled Miss Ellis. *Oh, help her to be happy more often!*

The hall bell sounded the end of another school day, and soon all the children had bidden Miss Ellis good-bye as they hurried from the room.

All but one. All but Dory. She stood very still, as if clinging to a magic moment for as long as possible. The lights had flickered out of her eyes, and her face seemed whiter than ever before.

Miss Ellis knelt and took Dory's cold little hands in her own. "What is it, Dory? Don't you want to be a special angel, after all?"

"I do, I do—" Dory's voice broke. "But—but—I'll be a horrid hunchbacked angel. Everyone will stare at me and laugh because angels are straight and beauti—" Dory's small body shook with uncontrollable sobs.

"Listen to me, Dory," Miss Ellis began slowly. "You are going to be my special angel. Somehow I'm going to make you look straight and beautiful, like real angels. Will you just be happy, Dory, and let me plan it all out? Then I'll tell you all about it."

Dory lifted her head hopefully. "Do you think you can, Miss Ellis, do you think you can?"

"I know I can, Dory. Smile now, you're so pretty when you smile. And say over and over, 'God loves me, God loves me.' That will make you want to smile. Will you try it, Dory?"

A shadow of disbelief crossed Dory's face. Then she brightened with resolution.

"I'll say it, Miss Ellis, and if you can make me look like a straight angel, I'll try to believe it."

"That's the spirit, Dory. Good-bye, now, and have nice dreams tonight."

Dory went to the door, paused a moment, then turned again to Miss Ellis.

"Yes, Dory, is there something else?"

Dory hesitated for a long while. Then she said slowly, "Do you think I could look like a tall angel too? I'm smaller than anyone else because my back is so bent. Do you think I could look like a tall angel?"

"I'm sure we can make you look tall," promised Miss Ellis recklessly.

Dory sighed with satisfaction and let the door swing

shut behind her. The silver bells on the Christmas wreath jingled merrily, almost mockingly.

*What have I done?* thought Miss Ellis soberly. *I have promised a little crooked girl that she will be a tall, straight angel. I haven't the slightest idea how I am going to do it. Dear God, please help me—show me the way. For the first time since I've known her, I have seen Dory happy. Please help her to be happy in Your love, dear God. Show me the way to help her.*

Miss Ellis went to sleep that night with the prayer still in her heart.

Morning came crisp and clear. Lacy frills of frost hung daintily from every branch and bush. Miss Ellis rubbed her eyes and looked out her window. The sparkling white beauty of the morning reminded her of angels. Angels! She recalled her promise. She had dreamed of angels too. What was the dream about, what was it? Miss Ellis tapped her finger against her lip in concentration. Suddenly, as if a dark door had opened to the sunshine, the dream, the whole angel plan, swept into her mind. Idea after idea tumbled about like dancing sunbeams. She must hurry and dress; she must get to the schoolhouse early to talk to Joe, the janitor. Joe could do anything, and she was sure that Joe would help her.

At the door of the school she scarcely paused to

stomp the snow from her boots. Quickly, she went down to the furnace room, where Joe was stoking coal into the hungry furnace.

"Joe," she began, "I need your help. I've got a big job ahead of me. I'm going to make little Dory Saunders into a tall, straight angel for our Christmas pageant."

Joe thumped his shovel down, looked at her intently, and scratched his head. "You certainly did pick yourself a job, Miss Ellis. How you going to do all this, and where do I come in?"

"It's like this, Joe," and she outlined her plan to him, and Joe agreed to it.

Miss Ellis went lightly up the steps to her fourth-grade room. She greeted the children cheerily, smiling warmly at Dory. Dory returned the smile, the candle flames of happiness glowing again in her eyes.

For Dory the day was enchanted. Round-faced angels smiled at her through the 0s in her arithmetic book. The time passed dreamily on whirring angel wings. At last school was over, and she was alone with Miss Ellis, waiting to hear the marvelous plan that would make her a straight and beautiful angel.

"I've thought it all out, Dory." Miss Ellis pulled Dory

close as she explained the plan. "Mrs. Brown and I are going to make you a long, white gown and wings, and Joe will fix you up so you will be the tallest angel of all. But, Dory, let's keep it a secret until the night of the program, shall we?"

Dory nodded vigorously. She couldn't speak. The vision was too lovely for words; so she just nodded and hugged Miss Ellis as tight as her thin arms could squeeze. Then she limped from the room.

Dory had never felt such happiness. Now she really had a place in the scheme of events. At least until Christmas, she felt, she really belonged with the other children. She was really like other children. Maybe God loved even her.

At last the night of the program came. Carols of praise to the newborn King rang through the school.

Finally it was time for the Christmas pageant. Soft music invited a quiet mood, and the audience waited for the curtains to open upon a shepherd scene.

The sky was dark as the shepherds sat huddled around their fire. Then suddenly a bright light burst over the scene. The audience gasped in surprise. High up on a pedestal, dressed in a gown of shimmering white satin, Dory raised her arms in salutation.

"Fear not." Her face was radiant as she spoke. "For, behold, I bring you good tidings of great joy, which shall be to all people." Her voice gathered conviction as she continued. "For unto you is born this day in the city of David a Savior, which is Christ, the Lord."

The triumphant ring in her voice carried to the choir, and the children sang, "Glory to God in the highest, and on earth peace, goodwill toward men," as they had never sung before.

Dory's father blinked hard at the tears that stung his eyes, and he thought in his heart, *Why, she's a beautiful child. Why doesn't Martha curl her hair and put a ribbon in it?*

Dory's mother closed her eyes on the lovely vision, praying silently, *Forgive me, God; I haven't appreciated the good things about Dory because I've been so busy complaining about her misfortunes.*

The sound of the carols sung by the choir died away, and the curtains silently closed.

Miss Ellis hurried backstage and lifted Dory from her high pedestal.

"Dory," she asked softly, "what happened? How did you feel when you were the angel? Something wonderful happened to you. I saw it in your face."

Dory hesitated, "You'll laugh—"

"Never, never, Dory, I promise!"

"Well, while I was saying the angel message, I began to feel taller and taller and real straight." She paused and looked intently at Miss Ellis.

"Go on, dear," urged Miss Ellis gently. "What else?"

"Well, I didn't feel my braces anymore. And do you know what?"

"No, what? Tell me."

"Right then I knew it was true. God does love me."

"Dory, as long as you know that is true, you'll never be really unhappy again. And someday, my dear, you will stand straight and tall and beautiful among the real angels in heaven."

Our Christmas Tree

# Pink Angel

✤

## AUTHOR UNKNOWN

*When God fashioned man and woman, for some strange, unexplainable reason, He instilled within each of us a yearning for appreciation. As toddlers, we grandstand from the first: "Look, Mommy! Look, Daddy!" Somehow, achievement unaccompanied by praise and recognition brings no sweeter taste than well-trampled sawdust.*

*In this little-known old story, Christmas is coming . . . and everyone wants to be noticed at once . . . but one is not—and therein hangs the story.*

There's always a special minute when it comes. Every year. Christmas, I mean.

Sometimes it's when the tree is up and trimmed and you step back from it and see it sparkle for the first time and hear it tinkling a little. And you smell that smell—of a piece of the woods brought indoors.

Sometimes it's a time when you find just the right present for someone you're very fond of and you bring it home and work over the wrapping. Or you get some special thing you never dreamed you would. Like that time I was emptying my stocking and I saw the box underneath it move and the cover push up and two green eyes look out and it was Magnolia, the black kitten. That was the minute that year. Often it's a song—on the radio or in church or once even the garbage man singing "Joy to the World" while he banged frozen-in grapefruit peels out of our can.

But it's always a minute that's special and then

Christmas is there. It's come for you. It hits you and leaves bells ringing in your ears.

It came twice for me that year. The first time was on a Thursday and we had only the next week and a half to go before vacation.

I had been feeling low ever since after Thanksgiving, when they gave out the parts for the Christmas program. My brother Pud came home all hepped up over getting a speaking part in his school play. My little brother, Bumps, was going to be one of the three kings of Orient. Even my tiny sister—she was going to be an angel in the Benjamin School play. Four rooms in her school and a little five-year-old kid gets a solo part. I'm the dumb one. The big brother in junior high, that's me. I get nothing.

Mother glowed when they told her. That's a nice thing about Mother. If you do something good, you sure get appreciation.

"Just think!" she said. "Such smart children I have. Some people have *one* smart one, one that gets into things. Look at me. Every single one. Jean, singing a whole verse of 'Away in a Manger' all by herself. King Balthazar Bumps, Innkeeper Pud." She looked at me. "And Rod," she said.

I laughed. I made it gay. "Yeah," I said, "and Rod."

"Well," Mother said, "playing in the orchestra isn't to be sneezed at. Playing a trumpet in an orchestra is fully as important as anything else," she said. But she swelled her voice too much on it. She was feeling sorry for me. She was proud of the others. She was sorry for me.

So it was her face lighting up that I saw on Thursday when Miss Phelps told me. Even before I got home, before I even told her, that's what I could see. Mother's face glowing with pride. Christmas had come. Only this time it didn't last.

It began to snow on the way home and that made everything perfect. I ran the last block. I would have flown if I could fly. Snow for Christmas and me with the lead in the Christmas play! I couldn't wait to tell it. *I couldn't wait.* Would Mother's eyes shine! It was too bad about Jim having to go to California, but *me!*

I stood for a minute by the door watching the snow, catching flakes on my tongue, trying to get myself quiet before I went in. I didn't want Mother to think I cared so much. I wanted to sound like it wasn't so much, me getting the lead.

I'd have to get a shepherd costume, a sheepskin thing they wanted, but Mother would do that. She was good at things like that.

"We must have a sheepskin someplace," she'd say, "under some of this junk around here," she'd say, and her eyes would be shining at me, hardly believing it. . . . She'd pooh-pooh the costume. "I'll get one," she'd say. "My goodness, for the boy with the biggest part in the play, we'll find a costume. We'll *buy* a sheep and *skin* it if we have to," she'd say. "Just you leave it to me."

I took a big gulp of the Christmas air and went in.

"Our program's Wednesday afternoon," I said. Just casual. Nobody knew I was the star.

"Wednesday," Mother said. "That's the twenty-first." She was piling cookies into a can. "Here, take one," she said.

It crumbled when I bit it. Pecans inside.

A lock of hair was in Mother's eyes and she pushed it away with her arm. She looked tired. She said, "Rod, can you come right home after school and stay with Jean?"

"Yeah, I guess so," I said. "Unless we have to practice." I took a big breath. "You see," I said, trying not to act excited, "I—"

"That's good," Mother said. "I've simply got to go downtown. There's Mabel and Lucile I haven't even looked for presents for yet. And Jeanie's presents for the neighborhood children. I'll have to take her along for that. And I haven't any of the family presents yet."

"I have a lot to do, Mother," I said.

"I know," Mother said. "Everybody's busy. It's getting so that's all there is to Christmas anymore. Rush, rush, rush. I hope Father can address cards tonight. He just has to take that over. When you come home, Rod, stop in at Rich's and see if you can get a box that would fit that stuff." She nodded to a chair full of packages in the corner. "I have to get that stuff off right away or it'll never get there for Christmas. Just think! Only two weeks away. It drives me crazy when I think of it."

About a week for me. A week to learn that part! It kinda drove me crazy too.

"Mother," I said, "I need a lot of time myself for—" But she was putting the can of cookies out on the back porch and talking.

"But not this noon," she was saying. "There's salad in the refrigerator. Get it out, will you?" She came back in and started putting dishes on the table. "We don't really have time to eat anymore," she said. "Where are Bumps and Pud anyway? Look out the window, Rod, and see what's keeping them. Jean, get your bib on and start eating. I should start you at eleven-thirty, the way you dawdle."

I gave up trying to tell her then. A thing like that you can't blurt out. I called my brothers.

They came in and dropped their jackets, and Bumps said, "I'll have to have that king of Orient's costume, you know."

Mother sighed and dried her hands on the towel by the sink. "Butter a roll for Jean, Rod," she said. "What do kings of Orient wear? Bright colors, mostly, I guess. I'll look in the trunk. I know!" she said then. "Maybe I can borrow that bright blue flannel peignoir of Barbara's and work it from there."

"What's a peignoir?" Bumps said. "I'm not going to wear girl's clothes!"

"It's a robe," Mother said. "Kings have to wear robes. Don't worry. I'll figure out something real kingly. I always do, don't I? Why couldn't you have been one of the singers—in everyday clothes. Why did you all have to be so talented, you smart children you!" She grinned. "Making so much work! I have to think up kings' costumes while I'm pushing through crowds looking for some nice little thing for the woman who was so nice to us last summer."

My, she didn't have time to listen to me tell about getting the lead, much less find a costume for me. You couldn't help being sorry Mother was so busy she had to eat on the run. But it made you kind of mad too. That she had to be so busy when you had such an important thing to tell. So busy she couldn't stop long enough to hear. My—this was big stuff. This was *big*. Not just a verse of a song. Not just a speaking part, not just a king of Orient. This was the *lead*.

"You didn't have to send that woman up north a present," I said. "You didn't have to."

"Well, I want to," Mother said. "But it's that angel costume for Jean which has me whirling right this minute. Angel costume, indeed. They're balmy over at that school."

Jean's lip shook a little and she pushed a piece of pear around with her fork. Mother was pouring hot water over her tea bag in her cup. She put the kettle back on the stove quick and patted Jean's shoulder.

"Oh, don't worry, darling. I'll do'er," Mother said. "I'll do 'er up brown."

"Not brown," said Jean unsteadily. "Pink."

"Yeah, pink," Mother said. "You'll be the angelest angel in town. Just you push some salad into that angel mouth."

Jean's eyes were shining wet and she ate a big bite of salad.

"I know my part," she said. Her eyes were almost

dancing out of her head! For Jean it was now. It was the first time. As long as I live, I'll never forget that first time for me in kindergarten. The Magic Star-maker, that was me. I remembered, looking at Jean: how wonderful I felt when I came home and told it; how it was, that day. A sea of faces with clapping hands beneath them. And Mother in the second row. That's the way it would be for Jean. The Christmas tree would sparkle in the corner, the people would smell wintery and Christmasy, the excitement would be racing all around, and she'd be good and Mother would be watching! Oh, it's always wonderful, but the first time it's magic.

"I know it perfeck," Jean said. "Want to hear it?"

"Darling, I can't hear it too often," Mother said, and Jean dropped her fork and stood on her chair and sang it, bobbing her head with the rhythm of it, her long blond hair bouncing, her eyes big and dark and serious.

*"The cat-tle are low-ing, the poor baby wakes,*
*But lit-tle Lord Je-sus, no cry-ing He makes.*
*I love Thee, Lord Je-sus, look down from the sky*
*And stay by my cra-dle till morning is nigh."*

147

Sure hits the downbeat, Jean does.

"Oh, it's so wunnerful," she said. "Wasn't I lucky to get pink for my angel suit, Mother? They pulled the colors out of a box and Alice got blue and Gail got white, and pink was left for me and that's best." I guess we'd heard about it a hundred times, but Jean was still telling it with gusto. Mother was listening with gusto too, her face beaming at Jean.

So I decided to wait. I decided not to tell Mother my big news till later, till she wasn't so busy that having to find a shepherd costume would be the last straw. I'd wait till I was alone with her so I could have all that gloating for me alone.

Mother gathered up her dishes and put them in the sink and sat Jean down again. She kissed the top of her head. "Eat the lettuce," she said. "You're going to have an angel suit that'll knock their eyes out. You know what I found this morning? An old pink formal I had once. You're going to be a stiff little pink tulle angel, darling. Finish eating and I'll show you. Tonight we'll cut it out. It isn't the gown that worries me, it's those wings. But we'll figure it out. Do you know your part, Bumps?"

Did he know his *part*? Wait'll she heard about me. The whole lead to learn in a week.

148

❖

"Sure," Bumps said. "I just walk. Step and hold, step and hold. It's easy. You got something for the murr?"

"The murr?" Mother said.

"Yeah," said Bumps. "You know, 'Murr is mine its bitter perfume breathes a life of gathering gloom sawring sighing bleeding dying sealed in a stone-cold tomb oh oh!' "

"Oh, myrrh," Mother said. "No, I haven't. But I'll look around. Goodness, you make it mournful. Don't you know how to sing it?"

"I don't sing it," Bumps said, "I just march it."

"What?" Mother said, surprised. "I thought it was your rich voice you were picked for, but you just march it? It was your gorgeous physique and kingly carriage you got chosen for—well, well. And your costume—we'll see. . . . Pud, you stop at Benson's shop for sure and get that cloak you're going to wear so I can wash it tonight. Oh, Rod, you are a comfort to me! I like people whose talents run to playing trumpets in school orchestras in plain suits of clothes."

"Well"—it wasn't exactly a good opening for it, but—"Mother, I'm not going to play in the orchestra," I said.

"Oh," Mother said. A sharp little *Oh*. "That's too bad," she said. "But don't you care, Rod. It's fun just to sit and watch. We have to have watchers too. We have to have an audience or there couldn't be any programs."

"Well, I'm not going to—" I began, but just then Jean stood up and handed her plate across to Mother.

"See, I cleaned it up," she said. "I better practice my part again, Mother."

"Oh, you know that thing frontwards and backwards," Bumps said.

"I do not," Jean said. "We have to march too. We have to march up when they play the piano. You can't go too fast. 'The cat-tle are low-ing, the poor baby wakes—' "

Suddenly I saw red. What if she was little, what if I was the oldest? Mother was my Mother too. Why couldn't I even have a chance to tell her about me?

"Oh, keep still a minute!" I said. "Mother! I'm not going to watch!"

"Rod!" Mother said. "Let her practice her part! My goodness, it takes practice to march and sing like an angel." And then she lowered her voice. "She's little, darling, let her enjoy it. Remember how it is the first time."

"Sure," I said. I could wait. My news would blow her over when it came. I could wait.

I worked on it while I was staying with Jean. And by dinnertime I just about knew it. Mother came home with

Father, both of them loaded with packages, Mother's face sagging with tiredness. She sank into a chair and kicked off her shoes and closed her eyes.

"Poor Father," she said. "If I had to battle that streetcar gang every night, I'd give up. Get my slippers, Pud. Get Father's slippers."

"It's not quite that bad all the time," Father said.

"I'd like to fall into bed," Mother said, "without undressing. Thank goodness for automatic ovens anyway. We come home, open the magic door, and there it is— meat loaf and scalloped potatoes. All we have to do is set the table."

"That's wonderful," Father said. "I'll have to learn that trick. What number do you set it at to get turkey?"

"There's a little more to it than that," Mother said. "But I do have one trick I'm going to need you for tonight. I'll show you how. All you have to do is sit in the chair by the desk and put a pen between your thumb and forefinger and turn your back to us. There's a list and a pile of envelopes, and in about three hours time, presto— addressed Christmas cards all ready to go!"

I stacked the dishes and went to my room to study. I studied my part. As soon as the kids went to bed, I'd tell her. And when I told her, I'd know it. She could hold the book while I'd say it over. Nothing nice and average about me. I get a lead in the morning, by night I know it. I was doing it in front of the mirror without the book when I heard her call.

"Everyone!" she called. "Hey, come and look. Just come and look!"

Pud ran down ahead of me, and Bumps came banging out of the bathroom. Father had come from the study and stood with his pen in his hand. Mother was in the middle of the floor and there were pink scraps all around her and pink threads and scissors and pins in a box, and over at the far end of the living room was Jean.

My breath stopped. And for a second it was all pure Christmas—something you can't quite keep but only can remember a little. There was Jean, a fluffy pink glittering angel, too beautiful to believe. It went straight from the neck, the gown, clear down to her ankles, and her arms were lost in it, and it was like pink foam, like glistening spun sugar, ready to disappear; and floating above it, with sparkling wings just showing in back, Jeanie's wide-eyed face. I never knew she was that pretty. All creamy pink and her mouth a little open and her eyes round and big and dark and her hair a soft golden crown around her head.

"My, that's pretty!" Bumps said.

And Pud said, "Wowie!"

And Father said, "Oh, honey, don't look so beautiful or someone's going to steal you away from us!"

And Mother said, "Isn't she darling?"

And Jean put one hand over her mouth and drew in her breath in a little gaspy delighted laugh and wriggled her shoulders, and then Father said, "I'll get the lights, I'll get the camera, we have to have a picture of that!" Father took the picture and then my world went spinning.

"Couldn't they let you off from work, Father?" Jean asked. "Couldn't they let you off for a good program like that? It's gonna be awful good!"

"I don't know but they might," Father said. "I don't know but they'd almost have to. When is this affair?"

"It's two o'clock," Jean said, "but we have to come ahead of time. Two o'clock Wednesday," Jean said. "Of course, Wednesday. There isn't any school on Thursday, silly." Mother unfastened the angel gown and pulled it up over Jean's head.

"Wednesday?" I said, standing real still. "The twenty-first?" I said.

"Yup," Jean said, pulling her undershirt down over her stomach. "Wednesday, December the twenty-first at two P.M., and everybody better get there early to get a good seat. You better get there early, Mother, and then you can sit right in front."

Mother smiled down at her. "Hurry now," she said. "It's past bedtime for all of you. What's the matter with you, Rod? Don't stand there dreaming. It's late."

I followed them upstairs. I went to my room and closed the door. I put the copy of the play in the drawer of my desk and locked the drawer. It was a long time before I could get to sleep.

We practiced every morning before school. We practiced every day during school. We practiced some-times after school. By the end of the next week I knew it frontwards and backwards. I knew it sideways. I knew the leading part of the play in less than a week with nobody helping me. I knew it, but it wasn't any good. Nobody was going to see me. Why should I care? Who cares if I'm any good?

It was the way they had schools in our town. All of us in different schools, that's why. They didn't plan it for people who had more than one child. Jean went to Benjamin. Me, I went to Junior High. What did they care about people who had kids in Benjamin and West Side? People weren't supposed to have kids a lot of different ages. What did they care if the programs came the same day, the same hour? What was that to them?

I couldn't even tell her about the costume. I didn't know what to do about that. Maybe I was a softy, but I couldn't do that to Jean. I'd look at her at mealtime, jabbering away about their program, jabbery-happy, and I'd think about it. I'd think about how it would be if I was to say, "Hey, Mom, I've got the lead in our Christmas play. I've got the lead, Mom." I don't know how it would have come out. I don't know what Mother could have done about it. If she came to see me, it would break Jeanie's heart. I knew that. If she didn't come—it was better for Mother not to know about it at all than to have to know and not come. I kept still.

So on Monday Miss Phelps says I'm no good. "I thought you were better than Jim had been," she said. "You read it so well that first day. What's happened to you? Please try harder," she said. "Try to think how you'd feel if you were that shepherd boy who had to stay behind when the others went to Bethlehem. You're the one that's left out, the one that nothing big can happen to. Try to make it feel like that."

"Okay," I said. What did they expect of a just-average kid? What did they expect?

"And you'll *have* to have that costume by tomorrow," she said.

"Okay," I said.

I didn't care what I wore. I went up in the attic at noon and looked in the trunk. So, who cared what the shepherd boy wore? Who cared anyway? Sheepskin. What did they think? That people just had sheepskin lying around their houses?

There wasn't anything in the trunk. Satin dresses, striped pants, silk scarves. I bundled the junk all up and rammed it back in and closed the lid. It was cold up there in the attic, but I didn't care. I dropped down on the rug in front of the trunk and put my head on my arm, face-down. Maybe I'd catch cold so I couldn't be in the play. I didn't care. Christmas sure was a lot of bother and work. That's the way it is, I guess, when you grow up. I was getting old, was all. It's kind of tough, outgrowing Christmas.

Can't blame a kid for crying when he gets that blue. I felt better after a while. I sat up and wiped my eyes on my sweater and waited a few minutes before I went down so my eyes wouldn't be red. Mother thought I was hiding Christmas presents or something up there. It sure was cold. I couldn't find a shepherd costume and I didn't care. Maybe they'd take the part away from me. I shrugged my shoulders and put the rug up around my legs to keep them warm.

It was an old fur rug made from the hide of a cow or something, that Grandpa got once. I stood up and picked up the rug—it was just the thing! All I needed was a hole for my head. I took it down to my room and cut one and tried it on. It looked kind of sad after all, but I sneaked it out to school anyway. It sort of covered me up at least.

The teacher fastened it together at the sides and between the legs with staples. "Guess it'll have to do," she said. "It certainly doesn't look like a sheepskin, though." She sure looked worried. What was so important? Nobody was going to see it.

"Sometimes sheep are black," I said.

"Yes, I know," Miss Phelps said. "But this is brown— or red. Are you sure it was a cow? It has such long hair. And sheep are curly."

"Maybe it's a buffalo from the Western prairies," I said.

"If it was a buffalo," she said, "it must have died of old age. Well, cow or buffalo, it'll just have to do. You aren't supposed to look glamorous after all."

I certainly didn't. I sort of looked like an old buffalo

57

getting ready to die, with its hide getting too loose for its frame. I felt like one too.

We got the Christmas tree up that night and I could almost feel happy again, just looking at it. Every reddish-pink ball made me think of Jean in the angel costume. I was sure glad I hadn't spoiled it for Jean. After all, Christmas is for kids.

On Tuesday, Mother went to the West Side to see Bumps march the king of Orient and carry the myrrh in an old Chinese brass pot she'd borrowed and to hear Pud say his two lines. "They were wonderful," she told Father that night. "Just wonderful! Aren't we lucky to have such gifted children?" she said. "Bumps was kingly and steady and—inspired-looking. I was proud of him."

Bumps beamed. "It sure was hard to walk that slow," he said.

"I'll bet," Mother said. "And Pud was wonderful! You'd have thought he really owned that inn. You were wonderful, Pud."

"That's what everybody said," said Pud.

"And now tomorrow is Jean," she said. "My good-ness, what would I do if I had eight children? I couldn't take it, I'd be so worn out running from one program to another." Suddenly Mother stopped talking. "Rod!" she said. "I forgot. Oh, Rod! I forgot all about you. Have I missed it? What day is your program? I completely forgot."

"That's okay," I said. "It's tomorrow. You can't go to both."

"Oh, Rod," Mother said. "I did so want to hear you play in the orchestra. Oh, what am I going to do?" You should have seen Jean—she looked like the end of the world.

"Well, you have to go and see Jean," I said, and it was worth it seeing her come alive again. "Anyway," I said, "I'm not going to play in that old orchestra."

Mother sank back in her chair. "I don't know, Rod," she said. "You always do things right somehow. Every mother ought to have a child like you. You never complicate things, you never foul things up. You always make things come out right and I love you. You'll play in the orchestra for the spring concert, I know you will, and we'll all go to hear you. Wouldn't you like to stay out and come and see Jean be an angel? I'll write you an excuse. Why don't you?"

"I'd better go to ours," I said simply.

"That's right," Mother said. "That's right. You had

better. We wouldn't want anyone to think you were jeal-ous or anything because you didn't get chosen to play with the orchestra this time."

*Rod, you always do things right somehow.* I kept thinking about Mother saying that when I was getting my cow-skin on.

The teacher was extra-excited. "Please do your best," she said to me. "Do it the way you did that first day, the day you read it. Make it good, Rod," she said, "and then maybe they won't notice your costume. I wonder if it would help any to trim off some of that hair." So she tried it. It gave it more of a French poodle look, and Miss Phelps looked sad and said pleadingly, "Do your best, Rod, please."

*Okay, I will,* I thought. *I'm the one that always does things right somehow.*

It wasn't hard, I'll say that. It wasn't hard to act it. It was just the way I felt. I just acted me, the way I felt upstairs there in the attic the day I found the cowskin. I was getting too old for Christmas. That was for kids. I was left behind now. Left behind while Jean and Bumps and Pud went ahead and had Christmas. Left behind while the others went to Bethlehem to see the Baby King in the manger. I was the shepherd boy who'd had to get his own costume, who was left behind to tend the sheep so the others could go. My, it wasn't hard at all.

I even got weepy over it. Nobody wants to be left behind while others go on and see the miracle. Nobody wants to grow up, I guess, and take responsibilities, give up things so others can have them. It wasn't hard and I was doing it! I was doing it like a breeze. I threw myself into it, moth-eaten old cowskin and all. And I knew I was good.

I could see Miss Phelps in the wings. Poor Miss Phelps. I'd sure let her down until now. Her face looked droopy and ready to cry. Miss Phelps was dead on her feet, she was too tired and nervous. She'd had to wait through all the orchestra playing, through all the carol singing, nervous because I was such a flop. Now she could hardly believe it. I was good.

I felt sorry for Miss Phelps. She was like me. Nobody cared enough to help her. Until now, I hadn't seen her side of it. Well, I was grown-up now. I had to think about those things. It was a sad thing to miss out on Christmas, but you didn't need to spoil it for others.

Only I'd had that little cry when nobody was looking. Up in the attic on the cowskin. And I could cry here in the pasture after the others had gone and I knew I had missed out. I pillowed my head on my arm in the grass of the stage pasture and cried. It came easy. The rest might not be so easy, but the crying was. Next came the hard part. In a minute I'd hear the quartet singing softly up in the rafters: "Peace on earth——" And then would come the hard part. Then I'd have to raise my head in wonder and let it show in my face.

Out of the dusky background on a raised place, lights would come up on the nativity scene. The shepherd boy would see it after all and I'd have to show how wonderful he felt about it. I hadn't done it right yet. I'd been told often enough. I just couldn't make Nancy and Timmy seem wonderful enough to get all excited over. Not even all dressed up in Bible clothes and leaning over the manger with tableau lights and a fine screen in front of them. Not even with the wonderful animals Perry'd gotten from his father's market. Not even when the shepherds came and the wise men came. Not even in costume. I guess I'm just not made that way. I just kept trying to figure out whose bathrobe they were wearing.

Then I sat up like a shot. Something was goofy. Someone was patting my head! I sat up and turned around, and I didn't need to act to look surprised. To look dumbfounded! A glistening pink angel was patting my head, and my mouth dropped open and I was dumbfounded.

Jean!

And that's when Christmas came the second time. That's when the glory hit me. Hit me with a bang that burst my eardrums, with a blaze that split my eyeballs.

For just one second I looked everywhere because it was too much for me. I just couldn't get it. And afterward they said that was good. As if I was wondering where the music had come from, where the angel had come from.

And I saw Mother!

She was standing in the wings beside Miss Phelps. Was she ever glowing! Maybe she was proud of Jean, and Pud and Bumps. She was super-proud of me. Not just because I had the lead. That was small stuff compared to the other. She was proud of me for not spoiling it for Jean. She smiled a wonderful smile and motioned with her eyes, and I took Jeanie's hand and turned and looked at the tableau, and if that audience couldn't see the glory shining in my face, they must be blind. It was blinding me.

Sometimes I think that was the peak. I'll probably never again have Christmas hit me like that. Right between the eyes. I hardly heard Mother explaining how Jean's program wasn't very long and she felt badly about me being the left-out one and so she'd gathered her up, wings and all, and had come on over. How they'd told her then, and let them stand in the wings. How wonderful I'd acted, so wonderful that Jean had been taken in and had run to comfort me.

I was still standing there when they all crowded around, squealing and jumping and Miss Phelps crying and telling me our play was going to be put on at the museum—with the sheepskin lining of an old coat of Father's instead of the cowskin, Mother said, and even with Jean. Most people thought it was planned that way, with Jean.

It didn't worry me any. I could do it again. With Mother watching, I could do it easy. I was grown-up, I was good, and the bells were ringing in my head.

Maybe Christmas will come again like that some day. But it can never be the same. That will always be the peak—the year I grew up and got hit so hard with the glory of Christmas.

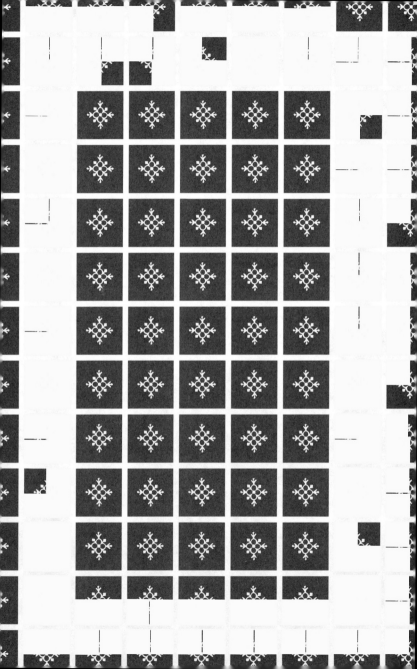

# Truce
# in the
# Forest

❄

## FRITZ VINCKEN

"It was Christmas Eve, and the last, desperate German offensive of World War II raged around our tiny cabin. Suddenly, there was a knock on the door . . ."

*Many have written in, asking that this memorable* Reader's Digest *"First Person" Award story be included in this series.*

When we heard the knock on our door that Christmas Eve in 1944, neither Mother nor I had the slightest inkling of the quiet miracle that lay in store for us.

I was twelve then, and we were living in a small cottage in the Hürtgen Forest, near the German-Belgian border. Father had stayed at the cottage on hunting weekends before the war; when Allied bombers partly destroyed our hometown of Aachen, he sent us to live there. He had been ordered into the civil-defense fire guard in the border town on Monschau, four miles away.

"You'll be safe in the woods," he had told me. "Take care of Mother. Now you're the man of the family."

But nine days before Christmas, Field Marshal von Rundstedt had launched the last, desperate German offensive of the war, and now, as I went to the door, the Battle of the Bulge was raging all around us. We heard the incessant booming of field guns; planes soared continuously overhead; at night, searchlights stabbed through the darkness. Thousands of Allied and German soldiers were fighting and dying nearby.

When that first knock came, Mother quickly blew out the candles; then, as I went to answer it, she stepped ahead of me and pushed open the door. Outside, like phantoms against the snow-clad trees, stood two steel-helmeted men. One of them spoke to Mother in a language we did not understand, pointing to a third man lying in the snow. She realized before I did that these were American soldiers. *Enemies!*

Mother stood silent, motionless, her hand on my shoulder. They were armed and could have forced their entrance, yet they stood there and asked with their eyes. And the wounded man seemed more dead than alive. *"Komm rein,"* Mother said finally. "Come in." The soldiers carried their comrade inside and stretched him out on my bed.

None of them understood German. Mother tried French, and one of the soldiers could converse in that language. As Mother went to look after the wounded man, she said to me, "The fingers of those two are numb. Take off their jackets and boots and bring in a bucket of snow." Soon I was rubbing their blue feet with snow.

We learned that the stocky, dark-haired fellow was Jim; his friend, tall and slender, was Robin. Harry, the wounded one, was now sleeping on my bed, his face as white as the snow outside. They'd lost their battalion and had wandered in the forest for three days, looking for the Americans, hiding from the Germans. They hadn't shaved, but still, without their heavy coats, they looked merely like big boys. And that was the way Mother began to treat them.

Now Mother said to me, "Go get Hermann. And bring six potatoes."

This was a serious departure from our pre-Christmas plans. Hermann was the plump rooster (named after portly Hermann Göring, Hitler's No. 2, for whom Mother had little affection) that we had been fattening for weeks in the hope that Father would be home for Christmas. But, some hours before, when it was obvious that Father would not make it, Mother had decided that Hermann should live a few more days, in case Father could get home for New Year's. Now she had changed her mind again: Hermann would serve an immediate, pressing purpose.

While Jim and I helped with the cooking, Robin took care of Harry. He had a bullet through his upper leg and had almost bled to death. Mother tore a bedsheet into long strips for bandages.

Soon the tempting smell of roast chicken permeated our room. I was setting the table, when once again there came a knock at the door. Expecting to find more lost Americans, I opened the door without hesitation. There stood four soldiers, wearing uniforms quite familiar to me after five years of war. They were *Wehrmacht*—Germans!

I was paralyzed with fear. Although still a child, I knew the harsh law: sheltering enemy soldiers constituted high treason. We could all be shot! Mother was frightened too. Her face was white, but she stepped outside and said quietly, *"Fröhliche Weihnachten."* The soldiers wished her a Merry Christmas too.

"We have lost our regiment and would like to wait for daylight," explained the corporal. "Can we rest here?"

"Of course," Mother replied with a calmness born of panic. "You can also have a fine, warm meal and eat till the pot is empty."

The Germans smiled as they sniffed the aroma through the half-open door. "But," Mother added firmly, "we have three other guests, whom you may not consider friends." Now her voice was suddenly sterner than I'd ever heard it before. "This is Christmas Eve, and there will be no shooting here."

171

"Who's inside?" the corporal demanded. *"Ameri-kaner?"*

Mother looked at each frost-chilled face. "Listen," she said slowly. "You could be my sons, and so could those in there. A boy with a gunshot wound, fighting for his life. His two friends—lost like you and just as hungry and exhausted as you are. This one night"—she turned to the corporal and raised her voice a little—"this Christmas night, let us forget about killing."

The corporal stared at her. There were two or three endless seconds of silence. Then Mother put an end to indecision. "Enough talking!" she ordered, and clapped her hands sharply. "Please put your weapons here on the woodpile—and hurry up before the others eat the dinner!"

Dazedly, the four soldiers placed their arms on the pile of firewood just inside the door: three carbines, a light machine gun, and two bazookas. Meanwhile, Mother was speaking French rapidly to Jim. He said something in English, and to my amazement I saw the American boys, too, turn their weapons over to Mother.

Now, as Germans and Americans tensely rubbed elbows in the small room, Mother was really on her mettle. Never losing her smile, she tried to find a seat for everyone. We had only three chairs, but Mother's bed was big, and on it she placed two of the newcomers side by side with Jim and Robin.

Despite the strained atmosphere, Mother went right on preparing dinner. But Hermann wasn't going to grow any bigger, and now there were four more mouths to feed. "Quick," she whispered to me, "get more potatoes and some oats. These boys are hungry, and a starving man is an angry one."

While foraging in the storage room, I heard Harry moan. When I returned, one of the Germans had put on his glasses to inspect the American's wound. "Do you belong to the medical corps?" Mother asked him. "No," he answered. "But I studied medicine at Heidelberg until a few months ago." Thanks to the cold, he told the Americans in what sounded like fairly good English, "Harry's wound hadn't become infected. He is suffering from a severe loss of blood," he explained to Mother. "What he needs is rest and nourishment."

Relaxation was now beginning to replace suspicion. Even to me, all the soldiers looked very young as we sat there together. Heinz and Willi, both from Cologne, were sixteen. The German corporal, at twenty-three, was the oldest of them all. From his food bag he drew out a bottle of red wine, and Heinz managed to find a loaf of rye bread. Mother cut that in small pieces to be served with the dinner; half the wine, however, she put away—"for the wounded boy."

Then Mother said grace. I noticed that there were tears in her eyes as she said the old, familiar words, *"Komm, Herr Jesus.* Be our guest." And as I looked around the table, I saw tears, too, in the eyes of the battle-weary soldiers, boys again, some from America, some from Germany, all far from home.

Just before midnight, Mother went to the doorstep and asked us to join her to look up at the star of Bethlehem. We all stood beside her except Harry, who was sleeping. For all of us during that moment of silence, looking at the brightest star in the heavens, the war was a distant, almost-forgotten thing.

Our private armistice continued next morning. Harry woke in the early hours and swallowed some broth that Mother fed him. With the dawn, it was apparent that he was becoming stronger. Mother now made him an invigorating drink from our one egg, the rest of the corporal's wine, and some sugar. Everyone else had oatmeal.

Afterward, two poles and Mother's best tablecloth were fashioned into a stretcher for Harry.

The corporal then advised the Americans how to find their way back to their lines. Looking over Jim's map, the corporal pointed out a stream. "Continue along this creek," he said, "and you will find the 1st Army rebuilding its forces on its upper course." The medical student relayed the information in English.

"Why don't we head for Monschau?" Jim had the student ask. *"Nein!"* the corporal exclaimed. "We've re-taken Monschau."

Now Mother gave them all back their weapons. "Be careful, boys," she said. "I want you to get home someday, where you belong. God bless you all!" The German and American soldiers shook hands, and we watched them disappear in opposite directions.

When I returned inside, Mother had brought out the old family Bible. I glanced over her shoulder. The book was open to the Christmas story, the Birth in the Manger and how the Wise Men came from afar bearing their gifts. Her finger was tracing the last line from Matthew 2:12: ". . . they departed into their own country another way."

# *Christmas Day in the Morning*

### PEARL S. BUCK

*What do you give to one you love very much . . . when you have nothing to give? This was the question Nobel and Pulitzer prize–winning author Pearl S. Buck posed in this oft-reprinted little story.*

*I'll have to credit my wife, Connie, for the discovery. In all the years I had known and loved this story, I had never real-*

ized there was a longer text than the one I had always read. She had already typed the indicated text onto disk but, before going on to the next story, she was curiously shuffling through the other copies of the story in the thick folder (several having been mailed to me by *Christmas in My Heart* readers). Then she stumbled on one that appeared to be longer than the others. Much longer!

Outside the window of our home, the snow was cascading lazily down in our first snowfall of the year. As she read the longer version, something began to tug at her heartstrings, she began to choke up—good as the shorter version had been, it had not been so to read it.

She brought it to me, knowing full well that her sentimentalist ol' husband would also be deeply moved. I was. Buck's early—and little-known today—version has great power, and is easily one of the greatest Christmas stories ever penned. The power that had been lost in the abridging has to do with a great truth: In order to give love, one must first receive such love from another. Every day in my classes through the years, I have interacted with large numbers of students from broken homes dealing with that heartbreaking reality: young men and young women unable to love because love was denied them at home (perhaps the most terrible price we pay for our "user-friendly" divorce laws). The price for such walkouts is never paid: It keeps getting paid again and again as long as time lasts.

*And so I thank my beloved wife Connie for her great gift to us all: Pearl S. Buck's original story.*

He woke suddenly and completely. It was four o'clock, the hour at which his father had always called him to get up and help with the milking. Strange how the habits of his youth clung to him still! Fifty years ago, and his father had been dead for thirty years, and yet he awakened at four o'clock in the morning. He had trained himself to turn over and go to sleep, but this morning, because it was Christmas, he did not try to sleep.

Yet what was the magic of Christmas now? His childhood and youth were long past, and his own children had grown up and gone. Some of them lived only a few miles away, but they had their own families, and though they would come in as usual toward the end of the day, they had explained with infinite gentleness that they wanted their children to build Christmas memories about *their* houses, not his. He was left alone with his wife.

Yesterday she had said, "It isn't worthwhile, perhaps—"

And he had said, "Oh, yes, Alice, even if there are only the two of us, let's have a Christmas of our own."

Then she had said, "Let's not trim the tree until tomorrow, Robert—just so it's ready when the children come. I'm tired."

He had agreed, and the tree was still out in the back entry.

He lay in his big bed in his room. The door to her room was shut because she was a light sleeper, and sometimes he had restless nights. Years earlier they had decided to use separate rooms. It meant nothing, they said, except that neither of them slept as well as they once had. They had been married so long that nothing could separate them, actually.

Why did he feel so awake tonight? For it was still night, a clear and starry night. No moon, of course, but the stars were extraordinary! Now that he thought of it, the stars seemed always large and clear before the dawn of Christmas Day. There was one star now that was certainly larger and brighter than any of the others. He could even imagine it moving, as it had seemed to him to move one night long ago.

He slipped back in time, as he did so easily nowadays. He was fifteen years old and still on his father's farm. He loved his father. He had not known it until one day a few days before Christmas, when he overheard what his father was saying to his mother.

"Mary, I hate to call Rob in the mornings. He's growing so fast, and he needs his sleep. If you could see how he sleeps when I go in to wake him up! I wish I could manage alone."

"Well, you can't, Adam." His mother's voice was brisk. "Besides, he isn't a child anymore. It's time he took his turn."

"Yes," his father said slowly. "But I sure do hate to wake him."

When he heard these words, something in him woke: His father loved him! He had never thought of it before, taking for granted the tie of their blood. Neither his father nor his mother talked about loving their children—they had no time for such things. There was always so much to do on a farm.

Now that he knew his father loved him, there would be no more loitering in the mornings and having to be called again. He got up after that, stumbling blind with sleep, and pulled on his clothes, his eyes tight shut, but he got up.

And then on the night before Christmas, that year when he was fifteen, he lay for a few minutes thinking about the next day. They were poor, and most of the excitement was in the turkey they had raised themselves and in the mince pies his mother made. His sisters sewed presents and his mother and father always bought something he needed, not only a warm jacket, maybe, but something more, such as a book. And he saved and bought them each something too.

He wished, that Christmas he was fifteen, he had a better present for his father. As usual, he had gone to the ten cent store and bought a tie. It had seemed nice enough until he lay thinking the night before Christmas, and then he wished that he had heard his father and mother talking in time for him to save for something better.

He lay on his side, his head supported by his elbow, and looked out of his attic window. The stars were bright, much brighter than he ever remembered seeing them, and one in particular was so bright, he wondered if it was really the star of Bethlehem.

"Dad," he had once asked when he was a little boy, "what is a stable?"

"It's just a barn," his father had replied, "like ours."

Then Jesus had been born in a barn, and to a barn the shepherds and the Wise Men had come, bringing their Christmas gifts!

The thought struck him like a silver dagger. Why should he not give his father a special gift too, out there in the barn? He could get up early, earlier than four o'clock, and he could creep into the barn and get all the milking done. He'd do it alone, milk and clean up, and then when his father went in to start the milking, he'd see it all done. And he would know who had done it.

He laughed to himself as he gazed at the stars. It was what he would do, and he mustn't sleep too soundly.

He must have awakened twenty times, scratching a match each time to look at his old watch—midnight, and half past one, and then two o'clock.

At a quarter to three he got up and put on his clothes. He crept downstairs, careful of the creaky boards, and let himself out. The big star hung lower over the barn roof, a reddish gold. The cows looked at him, sleepy and surprised. It was early for them too.

"So, boss," he whispered. They accepted him placidly, and he fetched some hay for each cow and then got the milking pail and the big milk cans.

He had never milked all alone before, but it seemed almost easy. He kept thinking about his father's surprise. His father would come in and call him, saying that he would get things started while Rob was getting dressed. He'd go to the barn, open the door, and then he'd go to get the two big empty milk cans. But they wouldn't be waiting or empty; they'd be standing in the milk house, filled.

"What in the world . . ." he could hear his father exclaiming.

He smiled and milked steadily, two strong streams rushing into the pail, frothing and fragrant. The cows were still surprised but acquiescent. For once they were behaving well, as though they knew it was Christmas.

The task went more easily than he had ever known it to before. Milking for once was not a chore. It was something else, a gift to his father, who loved him. He finished, the two milk cans were full, and he covered them and closed the milk-house door carefully, making sure of the latch. He put the stool in its place by the door and hung up the clean milk pail. Then he went out of the barn and barred the door behind him.

Back in his room, he had only a minute to pull off his clothes in the darkness and jump into bed, for he heard his father up. He put the covers over his head to silence his quick breathing. The door opened.

"Rob!" his father called. "We have to get up, son, even if it is Christmas."

"Aw-right," he said sleepily.

"I'll go on out," his father said. "I'll get things started."

The door closed and he lay still, laughing to himself. In just a few minutes his father would know. His dancing heart was ready to jump from his body.

The minutes were endless—ten, fifteen, he did not know how many—and he heard his father's footsteps again. The door opened and he lay still.

"Rob!"

"Yes, Dad—"

His father was laughing, a queer sobbing sort of laugh. "Thought you'd fool me, did you?" His father was standing beside his bed, feeling for him, pulling away the cover.

"It's for Christmas, Dad!"

He found his father and clutched him in a great hug. He felt his father's arms go around him. It was dark, and they could not see each other's faces.

"Son, I thank you. Nobody ever did a nicer thing—"

185

"Oh, Dad, I want you to know—I do want to be good!" The words broke from him of their own will. He did not know what to say. His heart was bursting with love.

"Well, I reckon I can go back to bed and sleep," his father said after a moment. "No, hark—the little ones are waked up. Come to think of it, son, I've never seen you children when you first saw the Christmas tree. I was always in the barn. Come on!"

He got up and pulled on his clothes again, and they went down to the Christmas tree; and soon the sun was creeping up to where the star had been. Oh, what a Christmas, and how his heart had nearly burst again with shyness and pride as his father told his mother and made the younger children listen about how he, Rob, had got up all by himself.

"The best Christmas gift I ever had, and I'll remember it, son, every year on Christmas morning, so long as I live."

They had both remembered it, and now that his father was dead he remembered it alone: that blessed Christmas dawn when, alone with the cows in the barn, he had made his first gift of true love.

Outside the window now the great star slowly sank. He got up out of bed and put on his slippers and bathrobe and went softly upstairs to the attic and found the box of Christmas tree decorations. He took them downstairs into the living room. Then he brought in the tree. It was a little one—they had not had a big tree since the children went away—but he set it in the holder and put it in the middle of the long table under the window. Then carefully he began to trim it.

It was done very soon, the time passing as quickly as it had that morning long ago in the barn. He went to his library and fetched the little box that contained his special gift to his wife, a star of diamonds, not large but dainty in design. He had written the card for it the day before. He tied the gift on the tree and then stood back. It was pretty, very pretty, and she would be surprised.

But he was not satisfied. He wanted to tell her—to tell her how much he loved her. It had been a long time since he had really told her, although he loved her in a very special way, much more than he ever had when they were young.

He had been fortunate that she had loved him—and how fortunate that he had been able to love! Ah, that was the true joy of life, the ability to love! For he was quite sure that some people were genuinely unable to love any-one. But love was alive in him, it still was.

It occurred to him suddenly that it was alive because long ago it had been born in him when he knew his father loved him. That was it: Love alone would waken love.

And he could give the gift again and again. This morning, this blessed Christmas morning, he would give it to his beloved wife. He could write it down in a letter for her to read and keep forever. He went to his desk and began his love letter to his wife: *My dearest love . . .*

When it was finished, he sealed it and tied it on the tree, where she could see it the first thing when she came into the room. She would read it, surprised and then moved, and realize how very much he loved her.

He put out the light and went tiptoeing up the stairs. The star in the sky was gone, and the first rays of the sun were gleaming the sky. Such a happy, happy Christmas!

# Tell Me a Story of Christmas

❄

## BILL VAUGHAN

*How passing strange it is that clarity of
vision blurs rather than sharpens with the
years. In this brief but poignant story,
a little girl gradually corrects her
father's inner vision: Without a moment's
hesitation, she steers a straight course
through mountains of pyrite to the
mother lode itself.*

Bill Vaughan *of* The Kansas City

*Star was known early in this century as one of America's premier columnists and humorists. But of all his prodigious output, it is this short piece that Star readers ask for year after year.*

*In my media interviews, few Christmas stories do I turn to more often than this one.*

"Tell me a story of Christmas," she said. The television mumbled faint inanities in the next room. From a few houses down the block came the sound of car doors slamming and guests being greeted with large cordiality.

Her father thought awhile. His mind went back over the interminable parade of Christmas books he had read at the bedside of his children.

"Well," he started tentatively, "once upon a time, it was the week before Christmas, all little elves at the North Pole were sad. . . ."

"I'm tired of elves," she whispered. And he could tell she was tired, maybe almost as weary as he was himself after the last few feverish days.

"Okay," he said. "There was once, in a city not very

far from here, the cutest wriggly little puppy you ever saw. The snow was falling, and this little puppy didn't have a home. As he walked along the streets, he saw a house that looked quite a bit like our house. And at the window—"

"Was a little girl who looked quite a bit like me," she said with a sigh. "I'm tired of puppies. I love Pinky, of course. I mean story puppies."

"Okay," he said. "No puppies. This narrows the field."

"What?"

"Nothing. I'll think of something. Oh, sure. There was a forest, way up in the north, farther even than where Uncle Ed lives. And all the trees were talking about how each one was going to be the grandest Christmas tree of all. One said, 'I'm going to be a Christmas tree too.' And all the trees laughed and laughed and said: 'A Christmas tree? You? Who would want you?' "

"No trees, Daddy," she said. "We have a tree at school and at Sunday school and at the supermarket and down-stairs and a little one in my room. I am very tired of trees."

"You are very spoiled," he said.

"Hmmm," she replied. "Tell me a Christmas story."

"Let's see. All the reindeer up at the North Pole were looking forward to pulling Santa's sleigh. All but one, and he felt sad because—" He began with a jolly ring in his voice but quickly realized that this wasn't going to work either. His daughter didn't say anything; she just looked at him reproachfully.

"Tired of reindeer too?" he asked. "Frankly, so am I. How about Christmas on the farm when I was a little boy? Would you like to hear about how it was in the olden days, when my grandfather would heat up bricks and put them in the sleigh and we'd all go for a ride?"

"Yes, Daddy," she said obediently. "But not right now. Not tonight."

He was silent, thinking. His repertoire, he was afraid, was exhausted. She was quiet too. Maybe, he thought, *I'm home free. Maybe she has gone to sleep.*

"Daddy," she murmured. "Tell me a story of Christmas."

Then it was as though he could read the words, so firmly were they in his memory. Still holding her hand, he leaned back:

"And it came to pass in those days, that there went out a decree from Caesar Augustus, that all the world should be taxed . . ."

Her hand tightened a bit in his, and he told her a story of Christmas.

# Luther

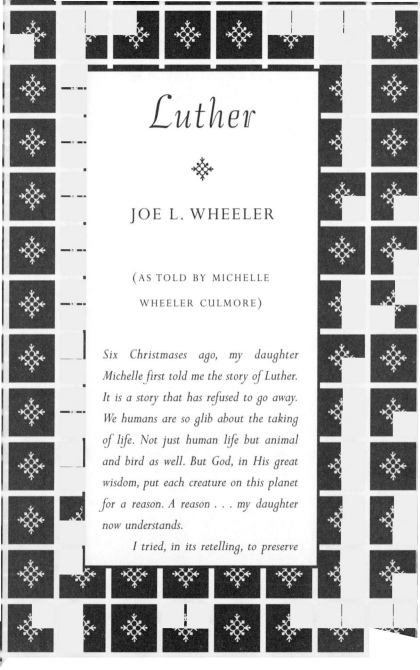

### JOE L. WHEELER

(AS TOLD BY MICHELLE
WHEELER CULMORE)

*Six Christmases ago, my daughter
Michelle first told me the story of Luther.
It is a story that has refused to go away.
We humans are so glib about the taking
of life. Not just human life but animal
and bird as well. But God, in His great
wisdom, put each creature on this planet
for a reason. A reason . . . my daughter
now understands.*

*I tried, in its retelling, to preserve*

*the natural rhythm of my daughter's original narrative. It is told*
*simply, naturally, just as she remembers it.*

Actually, it was a miracle that I ever met Luther, for he had been bought earlier in the fall to fatten up for Thanksgiving dinner. But something happened along the way to give him a Hezekiah reprieve: They fell in love with him—to have eaten him would have been like eating one of the family!

So . . . partly at least, to get him out of temptation's way, he was delivered to the theater to begin his dramatic career.

A senior fashion major, I was interning in a New England public theater, cutting my teeth—and other body parts—on costume design and repair.

Having always yearned to be in New England in the fall—*and* in the winter—the opportunity seemed almost too good to be true. When I arrived, it was to the lazy, hazy days of late summer, when the heat slows life down to a cat-like slouch.

But before long, the cooler winds of autumn swept down from Canada and all nature came alive again.

Soon it was "peak," as the natives label it, and all across New England the leaves turned to scarlet, orange, amber, and gold. Their reflection, in the sky blue of the lakes and rivers, took one's breath away. And spearing through the rainbow of colors were the soaring spires of blinding-white churches, legacy of those intrepid Puritans, three and three quarters centuries ago.

And then came Luther.

They sent him to stay at the theater for the remainder of the fall season. He came with his snow-white feathers, in a small cage with some plain dried food and a water dish. Not knowing what else to do with him, he was hauled down to the theater basement with the unwarranted assumption that the stage manager, Torsten, would somehow take care of him.

The theater basement was one of the places I hated the most. It was very, *very, VERY* dirty, damp, dark, and unorganized. I can't even *begin* to describe how dirty it was. Sort of a dumping ground for the theater: stage supplies, props, tools, trash, and remnants of the theater itself were strewn all over. And, like most New England buildings, it had been there a long, long time. It was even said that there was a resident ghost. If true, it surely slept a lot because no one I knew had ever seen it. Nor did I.

The basement was under the theater itself (duh), but was not paved or floored. It was essentially gravel, rocks, loose rusty nails, cement chunks, and who knows what else. One never went down there without heavy shoes on. When I remembered—and could find one—I'd wear a mask. Heaven only knows what toxic chemicals (asbestos, etc.) were staining the air—and it was grossly filthy to boot. Every time I went down, within an hour or so I'd get a headache, feel like I was coming down with a cold, and get a runny nose. And the grime in the air would rain down on body and clothes; in no time at all I felt filthy— inside and out.

I have to give Torsten credit, however. He did his best to fix it up during those rare occasions when he had spare time. As foul as it was, it was said to be an improvement on his predecessor's subterranean junkyard, one strata down.

Needless to say, imagine what all this did to the beautiful, clean goose—stuck down there for over a month! In no time at all he had lost his shimmering white beauty and had turned an ugly, grimy gray. And his health obviously suffered as well.

As if these conditions and the intermittent darkness were not enough, there were the kids—all one hundred fifty of them, streaming downstairs in hordes in order to get measured for their *Christmas Carol* costuming. They needed that many because there were two casts of children and a month-long run; out of the one hundred fifty, they hoped fifty a night would actually show up.

Unfortunately, we could process them only a few at a time—and that left them with time on their hands, waiting. To no one's surprise, they didn't wait well. In fact, it was bedlam! Just the memory of it gives me a headache.

Worse yet, it didn't take them long to discover Luther. They took turns playing with him, teasing him, taunting him, mistreating him. Amazingly, not once did he use that sharp beak of his to strike back—he just took it.

The staff wasn't much help either. Quite frankly, they were ticked that this unexpected responsibility had been thrust upon them. A not-unsurprising response given the fact that they were all overworked and underpaid—if paid at all.

So . . . Luther quacked and crapped (green, by the

way) all the time—most likely because he was in goose hell and yearned to get out.

I suppose he became attached to me because I was the one around the most, and consequently paid the most attention to him. I ended up being the one who fed and watered him most of the time. At that time we were in the concluding days of *Othello* and frantically—simultaneously, of course!—preparing for *Christmas Carol*.

Luther detested his cage and used his canny mind to the fullest in figuring out ways to ditch it—as a result, he got out often. And when he didn't get out on his own, the kids *helped!* During one of these escapes he cut one of his webbed feet on a rusty nail. Fortunately, Tracey (one of the actresses) had previously worked for a veterinarian. She was the only one (other than me, and, later on, Jay) sympathetic to Luther's plight.

We dug up some first aid stuff and tried to clean up his poor foot—no easy task when the grimy sink appears to never have been washed itself. There was nothing clean down there to ever set such a precedent! Then we put him in the shower (disgustingly dirty too, but the "cleanest" alternative around), and Tracey, costume, stage makeup, and all, got in with him. I locked the bathroom door (to keep kids and others out) and joined her in the cleaning process.

Unfortunately, she forgot she was supposed to go onstage when she was "called," nor was I there to help with last-minute costume changes and alterations, etc. The play went on without us (luckily for her, in that scene she was only an extra). But later on the director added a scene not in the script when he tracked us down after the curtain call.

Anyway, we used soap and shampoo to clean Luther up, feather by feather, layer by layer. He adjusted to this tripartite shower with such nonchalance, one would have thought these strange doings were part of his normal routine. We were a little apprehensive about what effect shampoo might have on the natural oil in his feathers, but concluded that few alternatives were worse than his current state. We then toweled him off (a process that gradually revealed light gray feathers), cleaned, disinfected, and wrapped up his foot as best we could, taped it, and he was free to try to walk. He was very cheerful about it all—except for the dubious looks he gave our bandaging artistry—and began cleaning his feathers.

The next morning he was white again.

And so Luther and I became friends.

Once he got to know me, he adored my petting him. He was most inquisitive, always wanting to know what was going on. Had he been a cat, he would have been purring on my lap; being a goose, he took second best and enthroned himself on the floor beneath my sewing machine.

And he was *very* vocal—I'd love to have a transcript decoding his end of our long talks together.

The bandage kept coming off—or snipped off, we never knew which—but we tried to monitor his recovery as best we could. He'd get dirty again and again and again. I tried to keep him with me as much as possible, but it was difficult—and more than a little annoying—as what went in one end promptly came out the other. In a steady stream. He never seemed to feel the need to wait for a "more convenient season"; consequently, I was continually cleaning up behind him, feeling much like a circus lady with a shovel in the wake of an elephant. Disgusting! Nevertheless, the process didn't seem to humiliate *him!* He followed me around everywhere I went in those downstairs catacombs, quacking indignantly as if to say, "Hey! Where do you think you're going? Wait up!"

As the *Christmas Carol* marathon began gathering

speed, and my work accelerated at an ever faster pace, I moved my ironing board, sewing machine, etc., over to the theater basement and into the backstage makeup room. Luther thought he had died and gone to heaven when I moved him in too, to keep me company. Maintaining sideways eye-contact (goose fashion), he quacked away with his stories hour after hour, stopping only once in a while to take a nap.

Then, as we neared zero hour, I worked there with Luther virtually around the clock, till I was hard pressed to avoid falling asleep at my sewing machine. Every once in a while I'd shake myself awake again, only to look down and see Luther eyeing me with puzzled concern and quacking solace.

Opening night came at last, but by this time I was almost too tired to care. Everyone else, however, was illuminated by that inner excitement that always accompanies first-night performances. Rumor was that a big-time city critic was going to be there, which added an extra edge to the excitement.

Soon I could hear the crowd upstairs. The milling around. The voices. And then the clapping. And after all the work I had done, I wasn't even able to sit back in the auditorium and enjoy seeing my handiwork. Here I was, still sewing, still altering, still helping to salvage or repair garments, during and after each scene. Before the winter street scenes it was a madhouse, putting mittens, hats, coats, and mufflers on all the fidgety children before their entrances onstage. As an added treat, just before the biggest scene, one frightened little girl, overwhelmed by stage fright, threw up on half a dozen costumes we had spent so much time mending, cleaning, and ironing. This created an even madder rush to find more costumes to replace them.

And then it was finally time for the big street scene, when Dickens's London was reproduced in all its vitality and diversity: with fifty children—all behaving now, wide-eyed and innocent—with several pet dogs and a pet ferret (one previous year, there had been a horse!). The entire cast was onstage at the same time . . . and Luther.

So it was that long before Tiny Tim's piping "God bless us, every one!" would bring that beloved story full circle, Luther had celebrated his acting debut by waddling across the stage. Noting how frightened he looked, Jay (head costumer and actor) leaned down and picked him up. Tenderly cradling his feathered (white again) body in his arms, and feeling the tomtom of his fast-beating heart.

From that refuge Luther contentedly looked out over the delighted audience and quacked out a soft "hello."

Sadly, I was not able to stay for the rest of the run. In all my last-minute packing and bequeathing of responsibilities, however, one worry remained constant: *After I am gone, what will happen to poor Luther?* We moved his cage to a far corner of the basement (actually, into Torsten's office). There was thus a cement floor and a door we could shut to (1) try to keep the kids from tormenting him, and (2) keep his lonely squawks from disturbing the audience. This room was much, much better than the first. But there he was, left alone. I felt terribly guilty every time I shut that door and heard him entreating me to come back.

As the last moments of my tenure at the theater trickled down like sand in the hourglass of my life, Luther began squawking nonstop. Actually, "squawking" is a totally inadequate word for what I heard. There is no one word in the dictionary that can begin to capture it; the closest I can come to is that it was halfway between an outraged squawk and a heartbroken sob. There is absolutely no question in my mind: He *knew!* Even though Jay promised to take care of him, I knew it would never be the same. It was heart-wrenching. It was terrible!

All the way back to Maryland . . . I could hear him cry: "Why, why did you forsake me? *Why?*"

I *still* hear him . . . on sleepless nights . . . on restless days. How this one little goose—nothing but soiled, once-white feathers, two inquisitive eyes, a quacking story that never quite got told, and a heart as big as all New England—can make such a difference in this hectic life I live, I guess I'll never understand. It just has.

That Christmas, Jay, bless him!—knowing I'm such a sentimental ol' fool—sent me a present. It was small, and my fingers shook a little as I opened it. It was a lovely ceramic ornament. One side was flat. But the other—the other side featured, in relief, a white bird. A goose. Luther.